Pre...

Katherine

_by_

Ashley

On the Occasion of

birthday 08/20/11

Date

Laugh Yourself to Sleep

OFFBEAT DEVOTIONS FOR THE "Unconventional" WOMAN

rachel st. john-gilbert

BARBOUR
PUBLISHING

Laugh
Yourself
to Sleep

Cover image © Dan McGeehan

The author is represented by WordServe Literary Group, Highlands Ranch, Colorado.

Published by Barbour Publishing, Inc., P.O. Box 719, Uhrichsville, Ohio 44683, www.barbourbooks.com

Our mission is to publish and distribute inspirational products offering exceptional value and biblical encouragement to the masses.

ecpa Member of the
Evangelical Christian
Publishers Association

Printed in the United States of America.

Dedication

To every woman who read *Wake Up Laughing*
and recommended it to others.
To new readers who fished this obscure
volume out of the Literary Ocean and didn't
toss it back in, I'm acutely grateful.

Contents

Acknowledgments

My biggest thanks goes to my mother and author, Ruthie Arnold. Mom truly midwifed this project, to the point of laboring alongside me in cyberspace during the wee hours the night before the manuscript was due. She rolled up her sleeves and even cooked up a few stories of her own making at my most desperate, sleep-deprived moments. "They won't put you in jail for plagiarism, as long as you have a note from your mother," she consoled.

Thanks to Dad, too, for letting me borrow his sidekick almost exclusively those last two weeks!

Thanks, too, to Tiff, Laura, and Beth for prayerful support of my Hermit Phase and the product wrought within my solitary shell.

I'm grateful for friend and author, Lynn Morrissey, who also breathed life into some of my earliest work on this project as I struggled to find my creative footing and hit my stride.

My husband, Scott, was awe-inspiring in his support of me, our children, and our home. On days when we all looked like we'd been struck by a Texas tornado, he had a knack for transforming us back into a Norman Rockwell painting. I know writers are prone to exaggeration, but this is no embellishment.

I'm also indebted to Rae Ann Boswell, the most patient, good-natured babysitter I've witnessed in a long time. Once she's moved to attend Auburn

University, the Dollar Store and CiCi's Pizza won't be the same.

Thanks to Brooke Broussard and Lari McCool who kept my preschooler, Whitney, happy and content at preschool twice a week (no small feat). Also, Jane Braddock and Sylvia McMahon shared not only their educational expertise with my daughter, Tori, but their big hearts and loads of patience with her harried mother. Contrary to appearances, I do own a comb and makeup. I can also tell time. . .when I remember to look at the clock.

Paul Muckley, senior editor for non-fiction at Barbour, has ruined me for working for anyone else. His professionalism in staying on top of details and communication, along with his enthusiastic encouragement took a lot of pressure off of every step in the process—from book cover to final manuscript approval.

Finally, thanks to Becky and Greg Johnson—two seasoned pros in the writing business. Your belief that my writing is worthy of coveted shelf space has meant the world to me. I'm in awe of your passionate commitment to each other and to those whose lives you touch. We'll take it one day at a time and see what the future brings.

I could not have persevered or finished well without each of you.

Love,
Rachel

Introduction
Confessions of a Pessimistic Humor Writer

It's with a twinge of tail-between-my-legness that I tap my initial feelings about the title of this book onto my keyboard. Although I was thrilled to be asked to write a sequel to *Wake Up Laughing*, the proposed title, *Laugh Yourself to Sleep*, had been keeping me up nights.

I could not shake the images of fluorescent yellow butterflies that advertise the sleeping drug, Lunesta, flitting about the country with the mission of wooing countless insomniac women to sleep, only to fly headlong into my book, suffering the same fate as airborne bugs whose lives ended haplessly on a windshield of a fast-moving car.

While I was nervous about linking laughter with sleep, other more important people around me were hunky-dory with it. The publisher thought of the title first. My agent seconded the motion, moving it a step closer to the printing press. Here were two heavy hitters in the industry who really liked the title. What other reassurance did I need? My mother's approval? Got that, too.

What to do, what to do?

Then it hit me. I would feel much better about the concept of women laughing themselves to sleep if I could get a consensus from those who woke themselves up laughing with my first book. So the publisher humored me (which was a good idea since I was losing my sense of humor), and I conducted an online "focus group" regarding the title. I tossed out several options and asked my reader friends to give me their best gut reaction. The results? *Laugh Yourself to Sleep* was the winner, time and again.

As the gray cloud over my head moseyed on to bother some other minutia-obsessed writer, I began to lighten up. *Wow! Maybe we're on to something big here. Maybe women don't need Lunesta and its butterflies to help them fall asleep after all. Maybe what they really want is a butterfly swatter in the shape of my book. Who would've thunk it?*

So here I am, newly released from title funk. I have to tell you, I'm raring to go. Chomping at the bit. So happy I could spit.

Here's to a little late night laughter for all of you unconventional women looking for a good time at day's end. I'll be right there with you. And I like to think that God will be smiling down on us all, rocking us to sleep with gentle (and sometimes boisterous) laughter.

Chapter 1

Earthy Humor

One afternoon my cute-as-a-bug, sly-as-a-fox sitter, Rae Ann, took my two girls on an outing to the local dollar store. Rae Ann, knowing three-year-old Whitney is tactile by nature (she explores *everything* by hand), showed her a small canister about the size of a Coca-Cola can filled with pink contents the consistency of, well—how do I put this delicately?—boogers.

"I don't want that," retorted Whitney, assuming in her vast life experience that this was nothing more intriguing than mere Play-Doh. "Just stick your hand in it," coaxed Rae Ann, knowing Whitney couldn't resist touching anything slimy, squishy, or furry. As Whit plunged her chubby hand into the canister, a loud "poot" sound emitted, and an even louder hoot resonated from deep within Whitney's belly, now shaking with laughter.

That evening at home, Whitney was giddy over her newfound sound maker and cackled with delight as she plunged her hand into the pink slime over and over again. She begged me to let her take it to show-and-tell at school the following morning. I had to think about that one, for fear that she might say the "f" word (for breaking wind) and get thrown out of our church preschool program.

As the evening wore on, even I—who am not usually amused by earthy humor—was overcome by involuntary fits of laughter regarding the pink canister of pooting goop.

Why is this so funny? I wondered, half ashamed of myself for falling prey to such lowbrow frivolity. Part of the answer came to me the next day while reading Dr. Terry Lindvall's book, *The Mother of All Laughter: Sarah and the Genesis of Comedy,* in which he wrote:

> *God made humans by mixing two very different things: divine breath and dust. Spirit and earth were sewn together into one patchwork person, a quilt with two different sides. On one we are related to the angels, the transcendent, the*

*spiritual, the Amish. On the other
we are cousins to jackals, weasels,
skunks, and lawyers.*

He goes on to share his own surprising experience with earthy humor:

*After radical hip replacement
surgery, I was convalescing miserably with tremendous gas pains in
my abdomen. Constipated and aching, I was attended by sympathetic
visitors, including my wife, Karen,
and my professorial friend Ben Fraser. Both of them had been praying
with me for a lessening of the intense
pain, when suddenly I was overcome
with flatulence. (These were, let me
tell you, no polite expressions of release but a volcano of unrelenting
praise from my southern hemisphere.)
When it was over, all three of us
laughed uproariously and thanked
God fervently. And everyone who
heard of it thereafter also laughed. Of
course, they also left the room as soon
as possible.*

It seems that sometimes when it comes to things of nature, including our bodies and their sounds, the Maker of all things bright and beautiful is also the maker of some things embarrassing and funny. So the next time you find yourself amused by something a little earthier than you care to admit, thank God for the humility that comes in being made "a little lower than the angels" as well as "cousins to jackals, weasels, and skunks."

As a father has compassion on his children, so the
LORD has compassion on those who fear him;
for he knows how we are formed,
he remembers that we are dust.
PSALM 103:13–14

Chapter 2

Trouble under the Golden Arches

It is with near amazement when I order a plain child's cheeseburger at McDonald's drive-through (clarifying "meat and cheese" only), then pass the booty to the back of the van, only to be met with the sounds of ruffling paper, followed by wailing and gnashing of tiny teeth. "Mooooom! It's got pickles and onions on it!" comes the tearful complaint from five-year-old Tori, accompanied by a stiffened body virtually standing in the car seat.

I was trying to calculate how many times I've had this spine-prickling Festival-O-Frustration of ordering a plain kid's burger and receiving one slathered in mustard, ketchup, pickles, and onions. Honestly, it's probably happened no more

than I can count on one hand, but because the epi-
sodes were so traumatic, I *feel* as if it has happened
a million times.

If, like me, you are a veteran mom, you
immediately understand that this situation presents
us with a double bind. Despite our weak smiles and
halfhearted offers to scrape the offending vegetables
off, we know that we are doomed before we can grab
the plastic knife for the culinary excavation.

Whoever decided to dice the onions into teensy
bits should be sliced and diced themselves. I can
still see those miniscule opaque cubes in my mind's
eye, hopelessly embedded in the melted cheese.
But this is only the beginning of the end. We still
have the matter of the pickles. Once removed, the
outline remains, like a fossil rendering every seed
in exquisite, maddening, light-green detail. My
daughter is convulsed in the throes of agony: "I can
still see the pickle print!"

I know you're thinking, *Hey, what's the problem?
Just check your order before you drive off.* Yeah, well, that
works for moms who have a couple of brain waves
still kicking around in their skulls. But after carting
preschoolers around town all day in the van (which
is the sole reason for the jaunt under the Golden
Arches to begin with), I'm basically brain-dead.

Moms like me only remember to check the
bag *after* we have let a foot off the break, just long
enough for the car behind us to advance to the

pick-up window.

As fate so often has it, by the time we open the bag, the drive-through is so busy that an unending line of vehicles is circling the restaurant—no doubt filled with frazzled moms, stiff-backed wailing kids, and ghastly bits of onions and pickles flying about the cabins.

Many times in life it seems we don't get what we order, despite our efforts. "One ordinary day, easy on the stress, please," we sigh heavenward. We may have even tried extra hard to be clear by employing an arsenal of communications aids such as speaking more loudly, slowly, or sweetly. And we still end up with those confounded onions and pickles mixed up in the cheese of our lives, making them icky and pungent.

Ah, life is full of joy and woe. We all get a mixture: our share of beloved plain meat patties and deplorable pickles in the paper bags handed to us from life's drive-through window. But I've found if I hand the bag to the Great Gourmet, He does a much better job at redeeming the disappointing contents than I can with my kiddy burgers.

In fact, God often takes my damaged *fromage du jour* and with His redemptive power turns a disastrous disappointment to a delectable delight. I may not end up with exactly what I ordered, but I find the chef's special of the day is always a perfect choice from One who knows best: perhaps a lovely

cut of character, served with a side of empathy, finished perfectly by a flambé of gratitude.

*I have learned the secret of being content in any and
every situation, whether well fed or hungry.*
PHILIPPIANS 4:12

Chapter 3

Creativity Rules!

Being a mom is a tough assignment at times, but it certainly has its rewards. One of my paydays popped up recently when our teen son, Trevor, brought home exciting news. He'd been nominated as one of the "most creative" students in his freshman class.

"Honey, that's wonderful!" I gushed, hardly able to contain my excitement.

"Yeah, pretty cool," he agreed but seemed a little worried. "The only thing is, I'm going up against Johnny Davis."

Even I, a lowly housewife, had heard of the legendary good looks and charm of the popular Johnny Davis. *Dear Lord, not Johnny! Can't we get a break here?* I silently whined—I mean, prayed.

I'd felt for years that Trevor had much to offer but tended toward shyness. He seemed content to let others take center stage. So I'd been praying he would someday find his niche.

I'd had a glimpse of Trev's lark side years earlier when his third grade assignment was to write a report about an American president and present it orally to the class. He was also to dress as his chosen subject.

Trevor, born a Virginian, chose Thomas Jefferson. Sparing no expense, we rented a slate-blue topcoat with tails, ruffled shirt, and knickers, topping off the ensemble with a powdered wig. One evening after practicing his report perfectly in our living room in full costume, he broke character and bounded over to the CD player. The '70s hit song, "That's the Way (Uh huh, Uh huh) I Like It," by K.C. and the Sunshine Band boomed through the speakers. If you've never seen Thomas Jefferson break dance, well, you just haven't lived.

So, as someone who appreciates humor, I hoped that once Trev entered his teen years, he'd get in touch with his funny bone and begin to tickle those of others. Then, just as his voice began to zigzag between falsetto and bass, he saw the movie *Lemony Snicket's A Series of Unfortunate Events*.

Amazingly, Trev realized that he, like Jim Carrey, could imitate a variety of dialects and he could recite lines from the movie, delivering near-perfect impressions. His newfound talent kept our family in stitches, and he apparently kept his classmates howling, as well.

That brings us back to his announcement in the kitchen.

Although my initial response to the news was to silently plead with God a few seconds, I managed to blurt out, "Well, it's a great honor just to be *nominated*!" and prepared a brownie snack for my "most creative" son, just in case he needed extra brain food.

Stiff competition aside, Trevor's nomination was one of those "aha moments" for me. It was validation of all the times in fourteen years when I had followed my intuition instead of my head in parenting this sweet-natured, bright boy. Many of his teachers had mentioned over the years that Trev seemed in tune with himself and others in a manner beyond his years. Now, seeing his peers recognize his emerging gifts seemed tangible fruit of my parental labor.

The following afternoon, I looked out the window and saw Trevor trudging up the grassy knoll of our backyard with his backpack overstuffed with textbooks. The Most Creative award was to have been announced that afternoon. Ready to ease what I felt would be certain disappointment, I wiped my hands hastily on my apron and ran to open the back door to give him a hearty greeting.

To my surprise, Trev was grinning like a possum; pinned to his shirt was a homecoming-style orange ribbon, declaring in gold-embossed letters: "Freshman Class Favorite, Most Creative."

Oh Me of Little Faith blurted out, "How in the world did you beat *Johnny Davis?*"

"I'm not sure," he answered, "but I think it may have been the 'Tom Carter Factor.' " Tom Carter was a "fringe kid," and although Trev wasn't buddy-buddy with him, he was always kind. That was his way with everyone. And now, the Tom Carters had come through for Trevor.

And that, dear friends, was even *more* heartwarming than knowing my son had been recognized as a creative genius! So, moms, don't give up. Listen to your instincts and make a comfy prayer closet—you may be spending lots of time in there until the harvest.

And let us not be weary in well doing:
for in due season we shall reap, if we faint not.
GALATIANS 6:9 KJV

Chapter 4

Nippy about Tucks

Okay. Fair warning. This will be a touchy subject in more ways than one, so let me *cut* to the chase. Once upon a time, the most emotionally charged debate among women was whether or not to work while raising young children. Nowadays, however, with the proliferation of makeover shows on the tube, the hottest suburban debate may well be "to tuck or not to tuck." And I'm not talking about your shirttail, either!

Admittedly, I've done my fair share of thinking about the nipping and tucking tug-o'-war. Will I or won't I? Now that's the million-dollar question— literally. As it turns out, it ain't cheap to buoy up your breasts or suck the lard out of your belly. This tomboy-woman somehow ended up with enough cleavage to put the *cleve* in Cleveland. Honestly, many times I've wished I could share the wealth with women who bemoan their flatter landscapes.

My pangs of longing for smaller breasts usually hit me (nearly slapping me in the face!) when I'm jogging. With wayward parts sometimes harnessed down by not one, but two, industrial strength sports bras, I try to make the best of it.

Of course the desire to whittle these wobbling wonders down also hit me every time I nursed one of my newborn babies with Hindenburg-proportioned mammary glands. Having three pregnancies under my belt (stuffed under) and having nursed all three offspring "till the cows came home" (*finally*—with homogenized milk instead of looking to me for their daily cream), I made a stark discovery. One morning as I stood unclothed before the bathroom mirror, I was shocked to see that my previously perky appendages had taken an oddly hangdog appearance. My breasts had gone from resembling two perky golden-retriever pups to a pair of aged dachshunds suspended nose-down the length of my torso.

Suddenly, I heard faint echoes of that old Girl Scout camp song: "Do your ears hang low? Do they wobble to and fro? Can you tie 'em in a knot? Can you tie 'em in a bow?" Well, I couldn't do it with my ears, but maybe. . .

A friend of mine recently had her chest "modified" and suggested I might go for a reduction consultation. At my age and stage in life, all I really want is a lift. So I figured it wouldn't hurt to get the low down on why my breasts were so, well, low-down. My husband, who, by the way, was not the instigator of this explorative exercise, teasingly called this investigation, "Operation High and Lifted Up."

The verdict? For me, for now, a lift is on hold. I'm not sure I want to trade my unblemished longitude for latitude with surgical scars. And there's also a not-so-small matter of a very large bill.

So I figure if the dachshunds keep defying gravity, I can either embellish them with rhinestone designer collars or throw them over my shoulders like continental soldiers. Who knows? They might appreciate a change of venue, and I might become a trendsetter. I can already envision the infomercial for "The Backwards Bra"; it could come in handy for women like me who don't know if we're coming or going half the time.

Nearly all women have body image issues. To avoid getting stuck on the Gerbil Wheel of Perpetual Cosmetic Surgery, it may be wise to make peace with most effects of aging and gravity. Some nonsurgical or less-invasive procedures may lead to an equally desirable result. Barring that, some resourceful women give their less-than-perfect assets an endearing nickname. Not a bad idea. Perhaps an even better idea is to give each other grace and space regarding this potentially touchy subject.

Now, if you'll excuse me, I'm taking Oscar and Meyer out for a jog while I thank God for the small and not-so-small blessings that are uniquely mine. At least for today.

In every thing give thanks: for this is the will
of God in Christ Jesus concerning you.
1 THESSALONIANS 5:18 KJV

Chapter 5

The Great Escape

Before I had children, one of my favorite things to do was travel. A change of venue is like a whiff of pure oxygen to this slow-of-pace-and-brain "creative type." Something about mountains, rivers, trees, quaint cafes, and whimsical art galleries makes my heart beat faster and puts a spring in my normally flat-footed step.

But, as I said, traveling was largely BC (before children), and now, as hard as I try, if I'm gone for more than a weekend from my adorable, exhausting offspring I begin to see their forlorn faces in every menu, mall, and movie screen crying, "Mommy, come hoooome!"

So it had been a while since I spent a weekend

away with a girlfriend doing what we pleased without consulting other needy souls. But that would soon change with the arrival of my friend Sally from Virginia.

In the weeks before her arrival, I was giddy with the prospect of losing track of time, getting wondrously lost in those moments of time, and making memories tinged with laughter, beauty, and personal epiphanies.

Sally and I decided to spend our time in Big D—Dallas, Texas. We would have three glorious days together, unfettered from the relentless responsibilities of family life. Can you say, "Woohoo!"? Can you envision:

- *Posh hotel*—French décor, luxurious well-equipped bath with white ginger soap and lotions—*Ooh, lah, lah!*
- *Pay per view*—*Sense and Sensibility* under cover of down comforters, goose feather pillows, and a queen-sized bed each to ourselves! (And no bored husbands snoring, mouths agape, to spoil the ambiance.)
- *Upscale snacks and fine dining*—Diet Pepsi and Almond Joy (*my* sense and sensibilities tell me that diet + fattening = still diet); girl-only dinners at trendy haunts; and coffee klatches at our every whim!
- *"Me" time*—Stacks of self-help books, mag-

azines, and requisite night-light.

- *Culture*—Dallas Museum of Art, browsing original works by Picasso, Monet, and Gauguin. Shaking up the security guards by whispering to each other across the gallery, "Did they say not to touch these?"
- *"Free to be me" chats*—Talking as only long-time friends can about anything and everything. Not having to weigh our thoughts, but letting them spill freely, knowing they are heard by an accepting, compassionate listener.

The only downside was the downpour—an unseasonably long and hard one. It was raining cats and dogs. Raindrops *kept* falling on our heads. A lot of them. During one soak-a-thon, I left to get the car, while Sally explored the sixth floor of the JFK Museum. I promptly got lost in low visibility and high volume traffic, arriving forty-five minutes late to pick her up from the gift shop.

By the time I arrived to save my Republican friend from Democrat overload—a mere five minutes from closing—I was too late. Sally had "crossed over." She emerged wearing a Kennedy baseball cap and sweatshirt, flagging me down with a navy blue mug embellished with gold presidential insignia. Her excuse?

"My sister is a big fan. . . ."

Yeah right.

Well, I *did* say that "personal epiphanies" would be part of our time away together, and while I expanded my cultural horizons in the Art District, Sally expanded hers in the political district, so to speak. (Those Kennedys *are* charmers.) What matters is that we expanded—not only our waistlines but also our personal horizons.

A few days and kids later, my friend and I were once again ensconced in our housewife lives of hectic schedules and bottomless piles of laundry. No matter. We *needed* that weekend oasis in the "desert of daily drudgery" no matter how fleeting. And what mattered more is that we reconnected with the fun-loving, fascinating interiors that lie just beneath our harried hausfrau exteriors.

How about you? Has it been too long since you've had an escape from your daily reality? We can't give to others if we have nothing left inside. Sometimes we just need a break. Other times we need an escape. Best wishes as you seek to stabilize your own internal equilibrium.

He has made everything beautiful in its time. . . .
I know that there is nothing better for men than to be
happy and do good while they live.
ECCLESIASTES 3:11–12

Chapter 6

Squirrelly Girly

Most women have a hard time keeping a pristine home unless they hire help to keep it that way. I often wonder if we worry too much about what others will think—we are so often our own harshest critics. Perhaps we would be a little easier on ourselves if we heard a different view.

My writing friend Susan lives in the country with her husband and three sons. Her boys hunt in the fields and fish in the creeks, so Susan doesn't have them underfoot too often. Even so, with her writing projects, speaking engagements, and travel schedule, her house usually leans more toward Rat's Nest than Pristine. In other words, if cleanliness is next to godliness, Susan hasn't got a prayer.

However, if lovability is next to godliness, Susan is a saint. Most of her friends, including me, love it that Susan's house is usually in a state of disarray. There's something freeing about never worrying about spilling coffee on—well, anything. Equally nice is that fact that we aren't tempted to compare our homes with hers and feel discouraged or jealous. We can prop up our feet and let the good times roll! Susan usually has us rolling right away with her storytelling skills. She is a walking treasure trove of "truth is stranger than fiction" funny stories. And the last one was a doozey:

> "I'd been to a Bible Study," she began, "and afterward my car wouldn't start. Well, Claire Smith—a new gal in town—offered to take me home.
>
> " 'I'd love to see your house,' Claire beamed. 'You know—where you write, how you manage with children.' I could feel the panic rising, remembering how I'd left my house that morning.
>
> "At the front door I tried to prepare her.
>
> " 'It might be a little messy. . . ,' I said. Reaching the kitchen counter, I cleared away cereal bowls and wiped up warm sticky milk as fast and inconspicuously as I could. Claire was still all smiles and seemed unmoved by the mess. 'Let me see what I have in the fridge

here,' I rambled. 'I think I have some cheese and grapes we could snack on while we visit. We'll sit out on the back porch. . . .'

"*My thought was to get Claire out of the house as quickly as possible, but when I opened the fridge, I gasped and shut the door in record time. I've encountered many interesting things in my refrigerator, but this time, even I was shocked. Staring me in the face was the carcass of a rabbit and the pelt of a squirrel. Obviously my sons had been big-game hunting.*

"*I took Claire gently by the arm and ushered her to the back porch.*

" *'Tell you what,' I suggested. 'Why don't you sit here in the porch swing while I fix the tray?'*

"*An hour later, we were fast friends, and I told her the truth about what was in the fridge. She laughed till she cried. Girls, Claire's gonna fit in just fine!*"

Susan finished her saga with this jewel. "Thank y'all so much for taking me just as I am—without one plea. Except, maybe, insanity."

"You know we wouldn't have you any other way!" I insisted. "Remember, *some* people say a clean house is a sign of a sick mind."

What is it about a "be yourself" kind of friend that is so irresistible? Maybe it reminds us of what unconditional love feels like. To be able to completely relax in someone's presence and home is a gift; and we can thank God for those who give us that relational luxury. We can even take mental notes and learn how to do the same for others when they come to our place. Maybe Susan can loan us some squirrel pelts to get us started.

For everything in the world—the cravings
of sinful man, the lust of his eyes and the boasting
of what he has and does—comes not from
the Father but from the world.
1 JOHN 2:16

Chapter 7

Sippy-Cup Silhouettes

One of my favorite things in all the world is a "sippy-cup silhouette." Nothing is quite like watching a toddler wrap both hands around a lidded cup, holding it like a football with a spout, and sucking the contents with the gusto of a man lost in the desert for days. Once detached from the vacuum-tight suction, his eyes appear slightly wet and red while he gasps for a breath of air, having been deprived of it for the long duration of that first sip.

For me, the sipping itself is cause for celebratory nostalgia. The sound of the juice passing through little lips and being gulped gently down tiny throats reminds me of listening to my kitten eat and drink when I was a child.

I would lie on the floor next to the bowls and listen to the sweet wet smacking of the kitten's pink tongue as it lapped up milk or fishy-smelling canned cat food. Oddly enough, this had a calming effect on me, similar to sitting by a stream taking in the sights and sounds of water bubbling playfully over rocks and tree limbs. Since we don't have a pet, and I do so miss the sound of their lapping, after my kids graduate from sippy cups I put their drinks in bowls on the kitchen floor.

I've wondered why I love sippy cup sounds and silhouettes so much. I think because I remember a time when a toddler was a nursing baby—helpless and completely reliant on Mom's milk and enraptured by her warm embrace and undivided attention.

At times I feel like a spiritual "sippy-cup toddler." My soul gets thirsty from being enmeshed in the relentless house chores, job assignments with endless details, approval hoop-jumping, personality conflicts, and the general fallout of living in a fallen world.

At week's end I am emotionally and spiritually dry, seeking a cool, satisfying sip of what the scripture terms "living water."

Indeed, Jesus gives us living water, and anyone who comes to Him will never thirst again (John 4:14). Maybe that's why Sunday comes at the beginning of the week. Maybe God knew from the beginning of time that we would need an entire day and night of rest from the crazy world we live in and from the fast-paced, multitasking schedules we keep.

Once we take a long tall drink of the "genuine" stuff of God's Word that truly satisfies our spiritual thirst, I wonder if we look like sippy-cup toddlers to God. Drawing in a deep calming breath, our eyes moist and even slightly red, we're fresh from the encounter with the God who cares. Perhaps God smiles at us the way we do at our own sipping kids—in wonder of our uniqueness and in deep love for the joy of our company.

"Be still, and know that I am God."
PSALM 46:10

Chapter 8

Somebody Start Me!

In a world of women with their gearshifts stuck on go, I'm more often stuck on stop. It's not unusual that my eyes glaze over and time stands still, and I find myself suddenly contemplating things as trivial as the shapes of pickle seeds or as paramount as the afterlife. Recently, however, my mind was going AWOL a little too often and too long—even by my own loosey-goosey standards.

The biggest indicator that something within me was slightly askew was that I was haunted by a daydream. *"Haunted?"* you may ask, a bit confused. "Aren't daydreams supposed to be pleasant?" Well, yes, they are. And mine was.

Too pleasant.

So pleasant that I wanted to run away from home and go live in my daydream. Its centrifugal force sucked me into it nearly every day, if only for a few mesmerizing moments.

I'm basically a simple person (can you hear my husband howling?). Okay, so my personality is as complex as the new government-subsidized prescription plan, but things that really turn my emotional clock and make its cuckoo bird burst forth in song *are* relatively simple. And thus was my daydream:

> *I saw a stone cottage with gray slate roof. The front yard was a wildflower garden, teeming with hues of lavender, coral, and white. Peppermint tipped tulips burst forth from the window boxes. Songbirds chirped in the spring-cool air. And I could hear the faint trickling of water trickling down a nearby stream.*

Pretty sweet daydream, huh? Sweet until it began to encroach my headspace too often (trust me, there's sparse room in that inn already). So several times a day the daydream would show up in my head and leave me with a sense of longing—and confusion. Longing to escape my real world of piles of paperwork, toys dotting the den, and needy little ones... In a matter of months, I became agitated by the increasing frequency of the daydream.

Then I secured the services of a life coach. During one of our sessions, Michele asked me to envision myself and my home in twenty years. Of course, my cottage emerged, in living color, it seemed, and I felt as if I were in the Vermont countryside.

Michele then asked me to describe the furniture and ambiance of the sitting room and to see myself as a woman of about sixty. She then gently asked, "Rachel, what advice would you give to a friend who had come to visit you?"

At this point I was pensive and melancholy. I began slowly, "I *think* I would say, 'Life moves on. . . faster than you think. . .and it's probably best to take as much joy along the way as you can.'"

I sat in silence for a few moments when the exercise was finished. Tears streamed down my cheeks.

In time, Coach Michele and Coach God helped me realize that I longed to bring beauty into my daily life. We began exploring ways to create niches for relaxation and reflection, as well as ways to link beauty with mundane tasks.

Weeks after I added a little "Vermont" to my home, something fascinating happened. The daydream stopped and healing began. I'm rarely pulled into the daydream now, although it does come floating back when life's pressures mount higher than usual.

Do you have a daydream or night dream that calls to you and fills your head and heart with images you don't know what to do with? Ask a trusted friend or spiritual director to pray with you, and ask God if He has a message embedded in those images. He may just want you to "take more joy," too—after all, life moves along faster than we think.

One thing I ask of the LORD, this is what I seek: that I may dwell in the house of the LORD all the days of my life, to gaze upon the beauty of the LORD and to seek him in his temple.
PSALM 27:4

Chapter 9

Proof Positive

While living in Atlanta, I visited a whimsical gift shop where I fell hard for a mug in the shape of a hyena head, with its ceramic face frozen in laughter. As I approached the counter, clutching my prize, the clerk turned out to be a silver-haired woman who was the spitting image of Grannie Clampett. She looked sheepishly at me over her spectacles.

"I wonder if you would mind pressing your thumb onto this ink pad and then onto the back of your check?" she asked. "Additional identification, you know."

"Wow," popped out of me, unbidden. "I've never seen *this* before." However, I obediently pressed my thumb into the slick ink pad.

"I'm sorry to have to ask you to do that but, darlin', we've had so many checks bouncin' lately," Grannie apologized.

This "system" seemed creepy, even though I understood it had been implemented to protect my bank account. I also understood it was an embarrassment for a grandma who was just trying to subsidize her pension. For me, it was too much like the cop shows I'd seen where a thumb was a tool used to book someone into the pokey.

What will be next as we "progress"? Will we be asked to step into a back room and pose sideways for a mug shot? *Sheese!* All I wanted was a mug, not a mug *shot*.

Feeling as if I'd been frisked, I stuffed the hyena into my purse and comforted myself with an afternoon latte. As so often happens, lots of unconventional thoughts flooded my mind.

Seriously, I said to me as I sipped, *what's next? What if they want my grandmother's maiden name? I'd be sunk. I only get it straight 50 percent of the time. Is it Smith or Jones?*

Maybe they'll ask to see distinguishing marks such as moles or freckles? My mind raced with anxiety, as I envisioned having to hike up my skirt to reveal the patch of freckles just above my right knee (even though the authorities would surely be impressed that the pattern resembles the shape of the little dipper).

With one final sip of the coffee bean nectar, I concluded: *That does it! I'm going completely to credit!*

But the soothing latte had its effect, and I began to get mellow and contemplative. I wondered if God sometimes shakes His head over *me* with the same puzzlement when I question whether or not I can trust *Him*.

I suspect that trust is challenging for most of us at some level. Otherwise, the ancient biblical scribes could have saved themselves writer's cramp and a ton of parchment by not bringing up the subject so often.

What should we do with our doubt? God has already given us a huge form of positive identification in the scriptures. He knows our names and personally reveals His trustworthy character in many ways. Even when there's been pain—and this is the hard part—*with the passing of time,* I can almost always see His purposes and the blessing He was preparing for me through the tough experience. If all else fails and we can hardly see straight through our current pain or make sense out of past pain, we *can* hold on to the hope that what we don't fully understand on earth we *will* understand in heaven. So, for now, I'll keep striving to make deposits in the Bank of Trust.

Laugh Yourself to Sleep

In his great mercy he has given us new birth into a living hope. . .and into an inheritance that can never perish, spoil or fade—kept in heaven for you.
1 PETER 1:3–4

Chapter 10

Timing Is Everything

Have you ever been in such an uncomfortable situation that your armpits transform into rain clouds, bursting into downpours of perspiration? You'd give anything for a trap door beneath your feet through which to disappear.

On one such occasion during the Easter season when we lived in Virginia, I attended a Maundy Thursday dinner. Various parishioners had graciously agreed to host it in their homes, adding a personal touch to the meal. I should add here that I had been accustomed to attending nondenominational, casual churches most of my life. But at that time I was attending a Presbyterian church and was especially intrigued by its architectural beauty and traditional choral music.

On the night of the dinner, I found myself at a lovely, colonial redbrick home situated on the banks of the James River. I was aware that homes in this particular neighborhood were either inherited or purchased by people of affluence. As I ascended the broad stone steps and reached for the brass lion's-head doorknocker, I began to feel like I was fishing for fellowship in a pond way out of my social league. I almost lost my nerve.

Mustering my courage, I grabbed the brass ring and boldly knocked on the massive oak door. A prim hostess, immaculately garbed in a yellow linen skirt and jacket, escorted me inside. I was relieved to immediately spy an old friend across the room.

"Harry!" I called out, waving wildly. Harry and I had worked together a few years earlier. We'd hit it off right away, discovering that we were both a little nutty and loved to laugh. He smiled and motioned for me to join him, saying, "I didn't know you were attending our church." He hugged me, and we each grabbed a mini crab cake from the antique mahogany buffet as we exchanged small talk.

So far so good for the country bumpkin turned Virginian Presbyterian, I thought, a bit smugly. Yes, all *was* well, until the hostess (or Mrs. Lemon as I had taken to referring to her while talking to Harry) offered the blessing. As she began, I noticed a slight tremor in her voice and was puzzled by her nervousness.

She poignantly gave thanks for Maundy Thursday, which led to Jesus' sacrifice on Good Friday. Then she prayed, "And Father God, we thank you for this glorious Christmas season, in which. . ."

As soon as the word "Christmas" slipped through the hostess's mouth, Harry poked me in the ribs. Our eyes met and I couldn't suppress a snicker. After she pronounced, "Amen," I, being a fun-loving Texan, thought I might ease the palpable tension she faced in a pin-drop quiet room. Making light of her mix-up, I casually said, "Hey, when do we get to open presents?"

Mrs. Lemon, now looking like a roughed-up canary the cat spat out, did not laugh. The other guests didn't laugh. Even Harry didn't laugh. Voluminous rain clouds gathered in my armpits, drenching my blouse in torrents of perspiration. My eyes fell to the floor, searching frantically for the elusive trap door. Harry had suddenly transformed into "one of them." He pulled me into the drawing room and whispered, "I can't believe you said that. Didn't you see how nervous she was?"

I've since returned to Texas, where the same comment in most of my social circles would have been met with good-natured chuckles. While my intentions were good, I learned a hard lesson that evening. I learned there's a time for solemnity and a time for frivolity—and a time for sensitivity. I also learned that sometimes, timing is everything.

Laugh Yourself to Sleep

We all stumble in many ways.
If anyone is never at fault in what he says, he is a
perfect man, able to keep his whole body in check.
JAMES 3:2

Chapter 11

What if God Was One of Us?

After reading Philip Yancy's book, *The Jesus I Never Knew*, I came to realize that Jesus experienced the full gamut of human emotions and wasn't shielded from their soul-stirring impact.

The scriptures indicate that Jesus was "fully" human. Yes, I know they also point out that He was also fully God, but I think we tend to blow right past the human part. It's as if we sometimes think of Jesus as being *half*-human, living like the Bubble Boy who couldn't fully engage in life or with people because he couldn't be exposed to germs (or in Jesus' case, sin and sinners). On the contrary, I believe when we study who Jesus hung out with while He was on earth, we find that He was quite down-to-earth and expressed a wide range of emotions.

Let's take, for example, the emotion of feeling, say. . .mischievously generous. As you may recall, Jesus was the go-to guy when the wine ran out at a wedding feast: "What? We mustn't run out of wine before it's time!" He must have empathized, realizing the celebration was in jeopardy of ending prematurely. Then, I imagine, with a twinkle in His eye, He feigned conservative restraint and said, "That's okay. Could you just bring me a hundred gallons of water instead?"

I can just see Jesus suppressing a grin as He waited for the first guest to sip His "water." Reminds me of those Gomer-Pyle people, like my husband, who just love springing surprises on the unsuspecting: *"Shaazam! Sur-priiize, sur-priiize, surpriiiize!"* I'm sure Jesus wasn't goofy, but He did love surprises.

Then there's the not-so-meek-and-mild Jesus. That side of Him got testy with charlatans who liked to use the church as a front to rip off the poor and innocent. As a Texan, I can see Him cracking that whip with "head 'em up and move 'em out" flair, like a cattle-driving cowboy boss in chaps and spurs.

Then there's sadness. He wept at the news of Lazarus's death and for the people of Jerusalem, who "like sheep have gone astray." He was, according to prophecies, a "man of sorrows, acquainted with grief."

Sounds like a regular person, doesn't He? Not some "semi-person" who was insulated from the pressures and heartache of real life.

Sometimes I think those old classic religious movies that show Jesus with those weird, staring eyes—looking spaced out on a mind-mellowing drug—have not been the best PR for God. I mean, who could really feel comfortable confiding her deepest thoughts, feelings, and fears to a space-cadet Jesus?

Thankfully, when the real Jesus comes to life on the pages of scripture, He's quite winsome. He was someone most of us would want to hang out with, or fish with, or. . .take a stroll *on* the lake with. Yes, He was extraordinary, but I think He was often extraordinary in *ordinary* ways—showing by example what love is all about.

Awhile back a popular song posed the question, "What if God was one of us?" The answer is that God *was* one of us. When we sometimes feel as if God is far away, it's good for us to reflect on who Jesus was during His life on earth. When we do, we often find that He was loyal, loving, and oh, so *likeable*.

Laugh Yourself to Sleep

*For we do not have a high priest who is unable
to sympathize with our weaknesses, but we
have one who has been tempted in every way,
just as we are—yet was without sin.*
HEBREWS 4:15

Chapter 12

Lipstick and Oil Slicks

On the day I began to write this book in earnest, the sun was shining and the air was crisp. Laptop in hand, I headed to one of my favorite bistros near a peaceful park. Yep, this was the writing life—having a bona fide excuse to be liberated from laundry, dishes, and children. Able to act artsy, free-spirited, and fancy-free. . .to write about life's little pleasures or important social issues like the spiritual implications of earthy humor.

After savoring each bite of my roasted chicken pesto sandwich and every sip of my black currant tea, I beelined to the ladies' room to wash my hands before attacking my laptop with inspired fervor. As I reached into my purse to grab my lipstick, I felt my makeup bag sticking to my hand.

"Oh no!" I moaned as I looked at a thin layer of a sticky black substance covering my entire palm. "*Great!* I must have a leaky pen."

Determined not to let this ruin my Bohemian mood, I simply soaped up a second time. Carefully reopening my purse to locate that pesky pen, I detected a pungent odor. Rummaging deeper into the bottomless cavern of my handbag, to my horror, I realized that I had somehow left the top off of a bottle of natural sweetener. The dark syrupy liquid had doused my belongings, with nary an escapee.

As I surveyed the scope of my situation, I laid out a roll of paper towels and began to fish out the contents of my purse. It looked like the Exxon Valdez oil spill, and I was on a rescue mission.

The irony of my plight was as thick as the goop covering my stuff: I had used this sweetener for its greater health benefits, and instead, now I was experiencing so much stress that it would take a hot-stone massage, a detox footbath, and a week of coffee enemas to undo the damage—not to mention the damper it put on my writing mood.

Here I was, all set to write inspirational humor in the vein of Steinbeck (oops, *Bombeck*) and now I was complaining under my breath in the ladies' restroom, wondering how on earth I could salvage my things.

Twenty minutes and a roll of paper towels later, I

had the situation under control. Although I smelled like prune juice, I thanked God I caught the leak before it had oozed out of my purse and onto my laptop.

Isn't that the way life is sometimes? A little leak left untended can wreak a lot of destruction. Take sin for instance. Satan tempts us with something sweet—maybe even something good for us like an inheritance or a job or a ministry. Then he leaves the bottle cap slightly askew. Before you know it, if we allow it, that something sweet becomes a sticky mess, and we're stuck in an oil spill of backsliding. We let our inheritance fuel our greed instead of our generosity; we spend more time on the job than with our kids; our ministry becomes all consuming and we lose our joy.

But God is on a rescue mission, and He offers a way of escape. He's good at capping sin if we'll let Him. When *He* cleans up our messes, He leaves no telltale residue behind.

But when you are tempted, he will also provide
a way out so that you can stand up under it.
1 CORINTHIANS 10:13

Chapter 13

No Laughing Matter

Although this book is entitled *Laugh Yourself to Sleep*, many women will read this at a time when they are more likely to *cry* themselves to sleep. I know this because I sometimes receive e-mails from readers whose worlds have turned suddenly, seemingly hopelessly, upside down through events such as a marriage crisis, debilitating personal transition, serious illness, addictive behavior, caring for aging parents, and even death.

I am currently navigating my own Humpty-Dumpty phase. It seems midlife with young children is cracking me up—and not in the comedic sense of the phrase. So I, a shell of my former fun-loving self, paid a visit to Dallas-based life coach

Michele Wahlder. I quavered to her, "The word that most describes my feelings is *frustration*—with a capital 'F'! I'm too old for this, I guess. At a time in life when I should be thriving, I'm only coping —barely. Life with little ones is just. . .*hard*."

Just in case you are more prone to tears than laughter these days, I asked Michele to share some of her own experience with pain and how she learned to not only cope, but to even thrive at times.

> *Six years ago, I was riding high on the success of a fulfilling career as a productivity consultant for a large technology firm. I left early one afternoon for a routine mammogram that revealed cancer. Just when I thought things couldn't get worse, the technology industry hit a downturn and two weeks after my diagnosis, I was laid off. I had no family living nearby, and my boyfriend became my major caretaker. Six months later, we had an impasse over a deeply held conviction of mine. Although I loved him and needed his help desperately, I felt I had to end the relationship.*

Michele's "Top Coping Tips":

- *Take acting lessons*—The sooner we start taking action for ourselves versus "reacting" to our circumstances, the sooner we'll stop putting our happiness on hold and feeling victimized. We may not be able to change life as it is now, but we become empowered by changing our attitudes.

- *Feather your friendship nest*—With a strong base of love, encouragement, and helping hands, most of us can make it through anything. During a time of crisis it's okay to set aside your ability to give (or give much) and exercise your ability to receive.

- *Accentuate the positive*—Look for people, places, or things to be grateful for throughout the day. Write them in a gratitude journal. It will redirect your mind and heart toward what is positive in your life.

- *Try "slow-mo"*—Quiet your mind and soul for at least five minutes each day, building up to more. Become an "observer of your experience," allowing whatever feelings and thoughts you have to emerge without immediately judging them.

- *Accept, don't regret*—Acceptance is not denying our pain but choosing to look at the reality of our situation as it is, rather than how we think it "should be." Accepting yourself, your current situation, and your feelings is the portal to peace.

- *Don't be an emotional Lone Ranger*—Share your feelings and thoughts with a supportive person who is a good listener. Other emotional outlets could include journaling, dancing, listening to music, or experimenting with different art media.

- *Become a "happy head case"*—Become aware of your "self talk."
  - o Write down any negative thoughts you are telling yourself.
  - o Write down a phrase that affirms the opposite of your negative thought. (Some people find it helpful to think of what their best friends would say to them.)
  - o Repeat the affirmations every morning upon waking or every evening before sleep, when the subconscious is most receptive to new messages.
- *Get moving!*—Even ten minutes of exercise a day increases endorphins and lifts spirits.
- *Help is only a prayer away*—When things look bleak, miracles are possible if we surrender our situation to God. One of the most powerful prayers we can pray when we feel stuck is, "Lord, I'm willing to see this differently."

Strengthen the feeble hands, steady the knees that give way, say to those with fearful hearts, "Be strong, do not fear; your God will come. . . . He will come to save you."
ISAIAH 35:3–4

Chapter 14

Good-bye Lullaby?

One of my favorite lullabies begins, "Hush, little baby, don't say a word." As a young girl, when I listened to the lyrics I remember thinking, *Lucky kid—her mamma buys her a mockingbird, a diamond ring, a goat, and a dog named Rover, for Pete's sake!*

Years down the road of life, at the end of a long day, my mind gravitates to that song when I'm singing my own young'uns to sleep.

The other night, as I perfectly executed the first line of the song with all the maternal warmth I could muster after barking at them all day, five-year-old Tori cut me off. "Mom, that song is for babies," she chided.

Babies? I thought with a combination of

defensiveness and sadness. She might as well have spat in my eye. I could have none of this—no child of mine would rain on my "Hush, Little Baby" parade! I rallied quickly. Wounded, but not fallen, I shot back, "It most certainly is *not* for babies! You haven't been listening closely to the words."

Tori rolled her eyes and slunk smirk-faced into my lap. However, her cranky demeanor was no match for this master lyricist, and before long, I heard her giggling.

Thus began our tradition of singing our own Loony Tune version of the great classic, "Hush, Little Baby," which is, most certainly, *not* for babies:

> *Hush, little baby, don't say a word,*
> *Mama's gonna buy you a cuckoo bird.*
> *If that cuckoo bird won't laugh,*
> *Mama's gonna buy you a tall giraffe.*
> *If that tall giraffe falls down,*
> *Mama's gonna buy you a scary clown.*
> *If that scary clown won't smile,*
> *Mama's gonna buy you a crocodile.*
> *If that crocodile smells funky,*
> *Mama's gonna buy you a spider monkey.*
> *If that spider monkey won't swing,*
> *Mama's gonna buy you a diamond ring.*
> *If that diamond ring ain't shiny,*
> *Mama's gonna pat your little heinie,*
> *If your patted heinie won't sleep,*

Laugh Yourself to Sleep

Mama's gonna buy you a flock of sheep.
If that flock of sheep starts to cry,
Mama's gonna poke herself in the eye.
If your mama's eye turns red,
Mama's gonna buy you a feather bed.
If that feather bed turns lumpy,
Mama's gonna get very grumpy.
If your Mama stays grumpy too long,
We'll have to go to bed and stop singing
     this song.

Lest you think I have rather strange tastes in lullabies, I leave you with my second favorite. This is another classic that I remember from childhood, sung, oddly enough, by the great-nosed comedian of the 1940s, Jimmy Durante. I can still see his eyes all bugged out and his rubbery schnozz wiggling as if it were made of Silly Putty when he shook his head for dramatic emphasis:

Skid-a-ma-rink a-dink a-dink,
Skid-a-ma-rink a-doo.
I love you!
Skid-a-ma-rink a-dink a-dink,
Skid-a-ma-rink a-doo.
I love you!
I love you in the morning and in the afternoon,
I love you in the evening and underneath
     the moon,

Laugh Yourself to Sleep

Oh Skid-a-ma-rink a-dink a-dink,
Skid-a-ma-rink a-doo,
  I love you!

Now I ask you, with lyrics this profound, who says lullabies are just for babies?

Sometimes all it takes is a little imagination to turn an otherwise routine endeavor into something with panache. When we find ourselves mindlessly doing "the same ol' same ol'"—whether singing the same lullabies to our kids every night or serving the same dinners week after week—we only need remember the adage, "Variety is the spice of life that gives it all its flavor."

If certain aspects of your life have turned bland, reach for the "spice rack" of your imagination and try a new flavor. After all, you can always go back to old favorites (perhaps with renewed appreciation) if you tire of the spiced-up version.

Sing to him a new song;
play skillfully, and shout for joy.
PSALM 33:3

Chapter 15

From Big Shot to Small Fry (In Zero to Sixty)

One of my favorite writing buddies is Jane Jarrell (author of *Secrets of a Midlife Mom* and *Simple Hospitality*). I love Jane mostly because she is one of the funniest women I know. I usually end up laughing to tears when I'm with Jane—no matter where we are or what we are doing.

I remember an author dinner at Sea World in Orlando. Everyone was milling about in a darkened grotto-type restaurant, with glass encasements where we could view sharks, sea turtles, and other ocean life while dining by candlelight. I somehow ended up without a seat assignment. By the time I figured this out, the awards ceremony had begun and dinner was served. I ended up hiding behind Jane's booth during the awards presentation, begging for bites of her pecan-crusted salmon (which she graciously fed to me at inconspicuous moments). Fortunately, her table was full of other humor authors, who good-naturedly tossed me leftovers as well. If this sounds too bizarre to be true, give Jane a call. My memory may be slightly off, but not by much.

Jane and I have shared both laughter and tears about our "riches to rags" stories. We strive to be open with other women about our struggles "in the dark," when we couldn't see even an inkling of light at the other end. In case you aren't familiar with my story, you can get the Cliff Notes in *Wake Up Laughing*, but in ways, I think Jane's story eclipses my own:

> *I was newly married and helping put my husband through law school. I was well on my way as a professional food stylist (I made food look irresistible by spraying it with shellac or intermixing plastic food with the real McCoy). I was beginning to write, as well, in the culinary genre, and also worked for Southern Living, presenting live kitchen shows across the country.*
>
> *However, one particular summer, as my husband attended classes, I worked at a historic plantation-style mansion. I was caterer to the*

rich and semifamous personalities who visited the small but prestigious college community where I lived.

Then one day I made a discovery that not only turned my stomach on end, but also my entire life. I learned that my husband had been unfaithful—with another man. Actually, with more than one man over time. Although I tried with every fiber of my being to restore our relationship, my husband was not willing to do the same. With tremendous grief, I ended the marriage.

As my world fell apart, I fell apart, too. I felt humiliated, rejected at the deepest level, and due to the divorce and pricey tuition, I also had several bills to pay. Finally, I accepted my brother's kind offer to come live with him in another state while I tried to put my life back together.

The next thing I knew I was employed at the local *Piggly Wiggly* grocery store, wearing a red smock with a wide-eyed smiling pig decal plastered across my chest, handing out *Little Debbie Snack Cake* samples on paper doilies. Thank goodness the pig was smiling, because I sure wasn't.

There's a saying that "Time heals all wounds," and I think that's partially true when it comes to grief. For me, the best saying *would be, "Time and Jesus and the love of special people heal all wounds." I am some fifteen years beyond those dark days now. I'm married to my best friend, Mark, and we share our lives with our precious, talented ten-year-old, Sarah, and soon to be equally precious and talented newborn miracle baby, Luke.*

It would be untrue and premature for Jane or me to write a message to you today that ends "and we all lived happily ever after." The truth is, we've each experienced significant pain since those "riches to rags" days, but nothing quite as acute and long in duration, yet. . .we have much living left to do. And life has a not so funny way of throwing us a curve from time to time, getting us off-kilter. But what we can say is this: Jesus lives. Jesus loves. There's a timeless praise song written by Bill Gaither that encapsulates the comfort in these two-word sentences. The song is called simply, "Because He Lives." Gaither tells us the simple fact that Jesus lives means we can face our fears head-on, as well as tomorrow. And that life is worth living, if *only* because. . .He lives.

Let us come boldly unto the throne of grace, that we may obtain mercy, and find grace to help in time of need.
HEBREWS 4:16 KJV

Chapter 16

Girly Man

How would you like to spend a weekend in a historic small town with B&Bs, trendy eateries, and quaint shops? When you're done sampling the local flavor, you can relax by strolling along the lake that runs through town.

Sound good?

Welcome to Granbury, Texas. And don't miss the red-hot show that draws packed audiences every weekend from nearby cities like Fort Worth. "Granbury Live!" is a variety show with the MC proudly announcing, "You can bring your grammaw or your young'uns anytime, and you don't have to worry 'bout 'em being shocked or insulted!"

Our friend Carey Dyer is one of the stars of the

show, a performer extraordinaire who shines on the stage. Billed as "the man with a thousand voices," he wows his audiences with impressions of Elvis, Sonny *and* Cher, Louie Armstrong, and anybody else he sets his voice to mimic.

But meet Carey at the grocery store or at church, and you'd never suspect he was such a talented showman. He has remarkably good manners, an infectious smile, and quiet humility. *Quiet humility?* Yes, he's a long-time friend of my folks, but to this day has a hard time calling my mom by her first name.

One evening over dinner with Carey and his wife, Dena, we talked about people with unisex names—those that can be worn equally well by guys or gals. Carey, who bears a unisex name himself, had a great story to share.

"Would you believe I received an invitation to participate in the National American Miss Pageant? It's true," Carey insisted, his voice rising to girlish falsetto while waving a pink brochure. "It's all right here!"

"Impressive," Scott crooned in his best girly voice. "*Do* go on."

"Well," Carey simpered, "I couldn't resist seeing if I have what it takes to be the 'next fresh face of the future.'" He handed the brochure to us. Blondes, brunettes, and redheads in sequined evening gowns sparkled from its pages. The last section detailed "Traits of a Winning Girl." Carey started checking off his qualifications with a pencil while we listened in—more than willing to help, *and* keep him honest.

"I'm faithful and patriotic," he announced confidently, while checking the first box.

"So far, so good," we all agreed.

"I'm friendly and caring."

"Oh, yes! Definitely," we chorused.

"I'm a girl with big dreams."

"Just one chromosome short on this one," Scott (ever the stickler for details) pointed out.

"Do you think they'll notice? I mean, come on now, I do have *big* dreams, and they did invite me to participate," Carey shot back.

"You nut," Scott replied, laughing. "Of course you have big dreams, but you're missing some other big, ummmm. . .*criteria*. Yeah, I think they'll notice!"

"You didn't really enter this thing, did you?" I asked, now half wondering if he might have mailed in the brochure just to see how far he would get for the sake of a good story.

"Nah," he said with feigned regret, "I mean, who has the time? Plus, the cost of one evening gown alone. . ."

While most blunders can simply be fodder for a hearty laugh, others may present temptations to unjustly take advantage of a situation. Each of us has our own unique personality bents and convictions, but when in doubt, the wisest decision may be to err on the side of being a Goody Two-Shoes. Then at least we'll feel something akin to the pride we felt as youngsters whenever we got to be teacher's pet. No doubt, we'll please the most important teacher of all, if we seek to please Him in the situation.

And what doth the LORD require of thee,
but to do justly, and to love mercy,
and to walk humbly with thy God?
MICAH 6:8 KJV

Chapter 17

Hit Me with Your Best Shot

I remember the dread I felt as a child when I had to get my school shots. My older brother would scream and flail so much that it usually required an extra nurse or two to hold him still. I, however, was stoic. When the needle was inserted, I simply turned white as a sheet and passed out cold.

Things did not improve much as I grew older.

When I was a new bride, my husband and I worked at the same university. I thought my weak-kneed needle days were behind me, but the human resources department took another view. I began to feel polite pressure to participate in a university-wide blood drive. I explained my iffy history with needles, but to no avail. This bloodletting had become a matter of corporate pride.

On the day of reckoning, I dressed for success in my navy blue power suit, complete with starched white shirt and red necktie. I marched toward the boardroom for my encounter with Countess Dracula, coaching myself all the way, *Come on, Rach, you can DO this.*

I sat in a leather chair and began deep breathing. I felt surprisingly calm and cool for the collection. *No sweat,* I thought smugly (at least none on my upper lip yet). Ever the jovial chit-chatter, I decided that part of my strategy to remain upright would be to play to my strengths and engage the technician in sparkling conversation. And then. . . the bell tolled for me.

"Ready?" The countess smiled, holding the needle in plain view.

"Sure," I responded with feigned confidence, silently thinking, *I wish she wouldn't wave that thing in my face!*

Once I was firmly in the place of no retreat, she became more subtle. "You'll feel a prick, and then you can just relax for a few moments. When you're done, you can have some graham crackers and orange juice. Beats working, huh?" (Little did she know I would have worked overtime as a welder in a shipyard in July to be released from her little shop of horrors.) The procedure turned icky right away as she thumped lightly on my veins, looking for the juiciest specimen.

Inexorably, the process continued. The vein thumping mixed with the sight of latex gloves and scent of alcohol made my stomach queasy. Seconds later, I felt light-headed. Desperate to stay lucid, I clung to my strategy of shooting the breeze with the countess.

"You know," I began, my voice cracking like that of an adolescent boy, "it's so silly, but I used to actually *faint* whenever I had to get a shhhh—"

When I came to, my husband stood over me, stifling his laughter. "Well, sweetie, you sure showed everyone you're a big girl now, huh?"

My eyes rolled into the back of my head, seeking peaceful repose. "Oh, pipe down and hand me my cracker and juice," I whispered with my remaining strength.

Of course, I was a young bride then. I wish I could say that as a mother I did better. But one day, three-year-old Trevor had to have an inoculation. Things began very well. My son sat calmly in my lap and took the shot just fine, while I tried to ignore the smell of latex and alcohol. While he proudly showed me his Ninja Turtle Band-Aid, the turtles turned fuzzy and began to look like ninja rabbits. Finally, they disappeared into oblivion—as did the room. The nurse noticed the telltale signs of a white face and beads of sweat forming on my upper lip.

"Mrs. St. John-Gilbert?" I heard a far-away

voice call. "Are you okay? Perhaps you should lie down for a moment."

While the nurse entertained Trevor, I convalesced from the trauma of my son's shot in the next room. Soon, kindly Dr. Blackwood, a father of ten children, appeared. He placed a cold washcloth on my forehead and gently patted my hand.

"Don't feel bad," he said with a smile. "I do the same thing when it's *my* kid."

At that moment, I loved Dr. Blackwood like a father. I was so embarrassed, and yet he was willing to humble himself and let me know I was not alone with my parental empathy pains. There's a lot to be said for empathy (when it doesn't render you unconscious). When we need encouragement or hope, nothing is quite as powerful as a word from someone who has "gone before."

A word fitly spoken is like apples
of gold in pictures of silver.
PROVERBS 25:11 KJV

Chapter 18

Accentuate the Positive

I was in my late twenties when our first child, Trevor, was born. I survived the first two years without a big hitch. The hitch came later as he approached the age of three.

Seemingly out of nowhere, Trevie developed a bad case of iron will. For example, I had spent many happy hours with Angel Baby at a McDonald's playland, clapping my hands with gusto every time his tiny tush slid down the yellow tube. But the closer he came to his third birthday, the "Playland Exit" became too emotionally charged for both of us, and I wasn't up to taking him as often.

The more Trevor exerted his will, the more I exerted my vocal cords. In spite of the parenting books I'd read, I took up hollerin' and bickerin'. I became a raving lunatic some days, while Trevor appeared virtually unaffected by my bulging neck veins.

Enter my friend, Karen Lindvall. Karen has a wonderful sense of humor and an easygoing personality, and was one of the best mothers of young children I'd ever observed. On one visit to Chez Lindvall, while deep in conversation with me, Karen began unloading the dishwasher. Without skipping a beat in our chat, she quietly, calmly confiscated a steak knife from two-year-old Caroline's chubby explorative fingers.

On another occasion, I marveled as she convinced five-year-old Christopher of the benefits of kiddy rides that didn't require quarters. Chris obediently fell in love with a stationary (and free) helicopter. Meanwhile, Trevor continued to demand quarters for action rides as if I had a direct pipeline to the U.S. Mint. Christopher and Caroline *did* whine occasionally, depending on what they thought they might be missing out on, but Karen was usually able to distract them—or confuse them with adult-speak.

I learned a lot from Karen's calm, determined demeanor. Her parenting style reminded me of the old adage, "You can catch more flies with honey than vinegar." She pleasantly stated her wishes, and her kids usually bought her viewpoint. This seemed to be a rather pleasant way to live.

Karen demonstrated to me that I could *learn* to be a relatively in-control-of-my-emotions-mom and still discipline my kids well. As a side benefit I could still respect myself at the end of a no good, terrible, bad day. So I tried yelling less and doling out consequences more. On the whole, it worked much better than I anticipated with Trevor, who is now a darn good teenager!

However, I'm now parenting two preschool girls in my midlife years, and find myself falling back into old habits. So I've taken up "whisper-yelling." It's a technique I developed after watching *The Godfather.* I really dug that raspy tone of his, and he seemed to command such respect, that I thought I'd give it a whirl.

Somehow I feel better about "whisper-yelling" than "yelling-yelling." Too, I'm thinking back almost ten years to a good friend with a wise head on her shoulders, and asking God to help me transition once again to the "Doler Outer of Consequences."

Funny thing, consequences. These days at our house when trouble's afoot and I've articulated what the lost privilege will be, guess what? *I'm* yelling less, and the *kids* are yelling more. The only challenge, and not a small one, mind you, is having the fortitude to follow through while the affected child is writhing on the floor.

We mothers know that some days disciplining

is so relentless that we feel like drill sergeants in sundresses. There are many different views on how best to deal with disobedient progeny. Most include some element of understanding the child's temperament and then applying an appropriate consequence to the infraction. Hang in there, because eventually the kids will begin to self-regulate much of the time, and as a payoff, you'll enjoy their company more.

A soft answer turneth away wrath;
but grievous words stir up anger.
PROVERBS 15:1 KJV

Chapter 19

Porky Pup

My parents weren't "pet people," but they did sometimes let us borrow the neighbor's kittens to dress in doll clothes. I have fond memories along the Beatrix Potter line, of dressing gray, yellow, and black kittens in pinafores and bonnets and rocking them as if they were real babies, their warm bodies lying against my chest, purring.

Eventually, my brother, sister, and I wore down our folks' resistance, and we acquired a six-week-old half-breed Pomeranian. He looked like a thistle, a round ball of blond fur with large glassy-brown eyes innocently staring at us. The saucy little tail curled over his back might have given us clues to his true nature, but alas, we were enchanted.

I called him Po-Po, my brother called him Wheezer, my sister called him Angel, and Dad called him Po-Po Deeny Schneeky. Under moments of duress, Mom unaffectionately called him Dingbat. It's no small wonder the dog was confused from the start.

He seemed to be a happy little fluff ball, but far from innocent. He was the canine counterpart to the mischievous monkey, Curious George. And my mother often played the role of the Woman in the Yellow Hat, chasing after him, cleaning up his messes, and apologizing to the neighbors for his incessant barking.

Among his most daring escapades was what we called "The Pork Caper." One afternoon, Mother had trimmed the fat off of a large ham and placed the trimmings in a plastic bag in the trash can under the sink. She then left for several hours.

When she returned, Po-Po bounded over to greet her, though she noticed he seemed a little heavy on his feet. Upon closer inspection, she noted that he appeared to be twice the circumference as normal. He resembled a porcupine on alert—body bloated, fur standing on end.

"What in the *world* have you been up to?" Mom asked, her eyes examining the family room for clues to how her dog had transformed himself into a blowfish on four legs. Before long she spotted a trail of ham trimmings leading from the family room to the kitchen. As she turned to scold the scoundrel, he keeled over at her feet.

Faced with the possibility that Dingbat was about to fly the coop to dog heaven, mother frantically scooped him up in her arms, tenderly laid him in the backseat of her car, and tore off for the vet's. There her rotund puppy barely managed to stand on the examining table, though weaving like a snake charmed cobra.

The clever vet defatted our dog and after an expensive overnight stay at the vet hospital, our Po-Po was back at home the next afternoon, begging for my ham sandwich. Did I mention he wasn't terribly bright?

As much trouble as Po-Po was, I could certainly relate not only to his insatiable curiosity but also to his propensity toward excess. We Americans are tempted 24–7 with eye candy designed not only to pique our curiosity but also to empty our wallets and keep us coming back for more. Images of gourmet foods, designer home décor, sleek sports cars, and all-inclusive cruises to white sandy beaches, appeal to the Curious Consumer George in all of us.

While we have a wide range of convictions regarding how much is enough, most of us know that uncomfortable feeling of being materially bloated. If we don't want to walk around feeling like Po-Po after his ham orgy, we'd do well to ask God to help us know when we've had more than enough of whatever our particular weakness may be.

> *"Watch out! Be on your guard against all kinds of greed; a man's life does not consist in the abundance of his possessions."*
> LUKE 12:15

Chapter 20

Incubators
(Not Just for Babies)

I used to feel like I had antennae on my head. Ideas of all kinds—from decorating to finances to writing—kept me up nights and occupied my mind during daylight, too! Soon I had too many ideas and not enough people to bounce them off.

In the first years of our marriage, my husband humored me and listened to a gazillion ideas and even encouraged me in a few. Some flew high like a Japanese box kite, and others flopped like a carp on the bank gasping for air. Before long I felt like the boy who cried wolf—too many sharings of my bright and not-so-bright ideas—and I had worn down the patience of my interested, or at least *listening*, husband.

I used to think I was alone in my idea-dominated inner world. But I have learned that lots of folks are like me—hardwired with extra antennae on our noggins. Yes, it seems plenty of brainstorming men and women out there are singing, "Don't Fence Me In."

I have a friend who happens to be a rocket scientist and who is, of course, an "idea person." Vince and I have a unique relationship. I don't understand most of what he says, and he laughs at my corny jokes. He earns his daily bread at NASA, working on payloads for space modules. As you can imagine, he's expected to come up with some really good ideas. He's in his element at work; think Albert Einstein on a good hair day. One day ten years ago I felt idea overload and a little worried about my entire, idea-driven psyche. So I dropped by for a visit with Vince and his lovely wife, Nancy.

"I know how you feel," Vince consoled while offering me a seat at the kitchen table. "Here, let me show you something." He grabbed paper and pen while Nancy ground fresh roasted espresso beans and served us homemade chocolate chip cookies. Nancy has her own touch of genius, as you can see. Vince, buzzing with energy and ready to enlighten, began tutoring me.

"A long time ago, I realized three important things about ideas," he explained, writing 1, 2, and

3 on the paper. "Together, these three simple concepts form a sort of Idea Incubator:

> *1) Loosen up—Hold ideas loosely. Not all of your ideas will be viable, but they may lead to one that is.*
>
> *2) Become a waiter—If your idea is not time sensitive, wait to share it with others. Then you can become discriminating about how many ideas you share, thereby not wearing out your willing listeners.*
>
> *3) Sit on it—Let an idea sit for a while. If it's a good idea today, it will still be a good idea tomorrow or next week or next month or even next year."*

Vince laid down his pencil. "Using this concept, maybe we won't wear out sweet-natured listeners like our spouses," he finished, winking at Nancy from across the table.

"Capital!" I slammed my hand on the table. "Why didn't *I* think of that?"

"Don't even go there!" Vince grinned, tapping his chest with both hands. "*My* idea!"

Vince's Idea Incubator has saved me a lot of wasted time and emotional energy. If you or someone close to you is an idea person, you can probably relate. When I let my ideas incubate and quell my racing mind, I give God a chance to be involved

—maybe even (dare I say it)—*in control.*

When we're creative, we reflect the nature of the Creator who made us in His image. Just a brainstorm here, but I'm guessing He might know how to bring out the best in those antennae He's bestowed on some of our overactive craniums!

And God said, Let us make man in our image, after our likeness: and let them have dominion.
GENESIS 1:26 KJV

Chapter 21

Pink Slip Blues

In the '80s, company loyalty went out of style right alongside muttonchop sideburns of the '70s. Corporate buyouts precipitated mass layoffs—rendering entire work forces irrelevant.

My own family's layoff experience was chronicled in my first book, *Wake Up Laughing*. We went from owning a new home, paying private tuition for college-preparatory kindergarten (I wish I were joking!), and leasing late-model cars, to becoming "suburban nomads." We packed up our "tent" (a 2-door coupe) and moved in with friends in Virginia, then to my parents' home in Texas, and finally to the apartment of a prolific roach with a southern drawl, er, crawl, in Georgia. We didn't actually pay rent to the roach, but he ran the place, or at least he ran around the place—quite a lot.

The first night we were in our apartment, my husband stepped out and bought groceries. I was so afraid that our money wouldn't last past a few weeks that I flipped my lid when I spied a jumbo box of Froot Loops and a super-sized bag of Doritos among the bare essentials.

We couldn't afford health insurance, so we joined the toothless, homeless, and hairless elderly at the public health center. Mercifully, our lot improved in a few years. Today I push those hard days to the bottom of my memory tank, but sometimes they float to the top like seasick guppies.

The "seasick guppy memories" popped up a few weeks ago when my husband came home from work, looking tired and *miffed*.

"Another one bit the dust," Scott announced, shaking his head in disbelief. "Dave got canned!"

"Ouch!" I said, half sad, half mad. Dave was one of our dearest, long-term friends.

"You know the drill. Health insurance issues alone could take him down if he's not working again soon."

Dave's company, Hearts Afire Ministries*, had a reputation for firing folks "on the spot"—no notice, probation, or mediation. Employees jokingly (and with some trepidation) referred to the company as "Hearts Afired."

Okay, so we Christians expect that from "the world." But the Pollyanna in us likes to imagine that some sweet Grandma runs most ministries and personally delivers paychecks from her handbag along with Tootsie Rolls on Fridays.

Many of you have had a ringside seat to Barnum & Bailey's Three-Ring Firing Circus: a time when you or someone you love is performing center stage at work, and then gets swept away by the crook of Little Bo Peep's corporate hook.

Well, don't get too down on yourself, because you are in good company! Here are just a few cases I've witnessed:

1) A single woman who dedicated the prime of her life to her company. Then, to quote a goat, ended up in a very "baaaa-d" situation: She became a scapegoat for management's poor planning.

2) A friend, with over twenty years of impeccable service, edged out of his position because of a personality conflict with a new hire who was higher on the corporate food chain.

3) A family member who refused to participate in a cover-up was transferred to a lower rung on the corporate ladder. In time, the cover-upper's "work" was *un*covered, and the good guy shimmied back up the ladder of success.

So, my friend, if the hook has swept you or someone you care about off center stage, you are not alone. And you may not be the party who is most at fault for the parting of ways. According to several top consulting firms, substandard communication by managers and inferior human resource policies are at the root of most on-the-spot firings.

Meanwhile, try to remember that at times, even among Christians, you'll encounter disagreements about the appropriate resolutions to sticky employment situations. In the end, forgiveness must rule the day. Life goes on, and God teaches us heart lessons that will make us wiser and more compassionate.

Even so, might I say, "Ouch!" and "pass the emotional Band-Aids—or tourniquets," whichever the case may be!

They had such a sharp disagreement that they parted company. Barnabas took Mark and sailed for Cyprus, but Paul chose Silas and left.
ACTS 15:39–40

* Hearts Afire Ministries is a fictional entity.

Chapter 22

Rainy Days and Mondays

Have you ever had a "downpour day" in which you wake up feeling ugly, the weather's cloudy and humid, and to top it off, you start your period (or your last child is headed to college and you *don't* start your period)? It's true that sometimes when it rains, it pours.

I was feeling the emotional humidity of a string of downpour days—feeling sorry for myself having to write for the third day straight at Chuck E. Cheese pizza parlor (with a giant rodent in red clown shoes crooning at top volume in the background).

Later that night while rummaging through research folders for devotional fodder, I ran across an old note and essay from my sister Becky while she was under tremendous stress. She had written it at a time when she had gone back to college. She was also raising four children and living in an 850-square-foot cabin that her husband had been renovating into a lakeside cottage—for the past *five years.*

Oddly (*sadly* really) the letter cheered me up. I wish it weren't true, but it seems nothing is quite as comforting as hearing someone else's woes to make mine pale in comparison. The letter began,

> *Hey, Rach! Not sure I'm collegiate material at age thirty, but I'm sticking with it. Small victory today: I got an A on a creative writing assignment. More later. I've enclosed my story, as thought you might relate. . .*

> *Love you,*
> *Beck*

Rainy Days and Mondays

> *On the morning I promised to chaperon Zeke's field trip, I woke up with a huge red pimple on the end of my schnozz.*

> *"Okay," I told myself. "So you woke up with a little pimple. All right, a huge pimple. You will not disgrace your son; you'll be the only*

one who notices it. You are blowing this tiny imperfection in an otherwise flawless face out of all proportion." And off I went to the field trip.

After inspecting six million specimens of amphibians and reptiles at the Museum of Natural Creatures, I was not feeling good about myself, as the "I Love Me!" support group would say. And that was before it began to rain.

At Burger Barn for lunch, I fell into the soggy line at the counter, jostled about in a sea of starving nine-year-olds. I caught a sympathetic glance from another field trip mom, although she looked better than I did. Actually she looked like Julia Roberts, while I looked more like Oral Roberts. This turn of events made feel me even crabbier. Still, she was the only woman within earshot, and I was so desperate for comfort, I turned to her.

"I just feel so ugly today," I ventured. "My hair's a wet mess. . ."

A bright-eyed boy named Christopher chimed in. "Yeah, and you've got a great big red mole thing on your nose, too!"

Releasing any self-respect I had left, I asked Pretty Woman, "Would you mind watching my group while they finish ordering? I have a volcano to spackle."

Thank God, Becky not only has a flair for drama but also a great sense of humor. She also has a knack for making the best of "when it rains, it pours" situations. And when the clouds gather in my personal Hundred Acre Wood, the Eeyore in me really needs the Tigger in her, so I'm thankful for her umbrella of encouragement, canopied in laughter.

Trust in the LORD with all thine heart;
and lean not unto thine own understanding.
In all thy ways acknowledge him,
and he shall direct thy paths.
PROVERBS 3:5–6 KJV

Chapter 23

Lone Laughers

Growing up attending a nondenominational Bible church, I remember logging many hours listening to skilled pastors and seminarians expound upon beloved passages of scripture. But even the most eloquent of expositors would occasionally get tongue-tied.

My family valued humor *almost* as much as faith, so when the preacher made a slip of the lip, one of us often hid behind his or her hymnal, trying desperately to gain control. Often the poor soul was the *only* one in the audience whose funny bone had been so dangerously activated. I was not immune.

One Sunday evening when I was a teen, I

listened to an esteemed graduate of Dallas Theological Seminary preach on Moses and his encounter with God in the burning bush. With all the drama Dr. Jones could muster, he held his Bible aloft.

"Moses!" he cried in his rich, beautiful voice, "Take off your feet! You're standing on holy ground!"

I began to giggle quietly at first, hoping I could stifle myself. My girlfriend, Lou Ann, was sitting beside me, and her shoulders began to quake.

So now I had company, but it only made my situation worse as I couldn't resist embellishing the blooper further. I regained control of myself long enough to whisper to my friend, "Bet he had a hard time getting down that mountain without his feet on."

My buddy and I snorted and expected one of our parents to appear and march us out of the sanctuary by our ears.

My parents, however, have had their own brushes with disgrace. On their first visit to a new Sunday school class, they heard the teacher announce that a group from Jungle Aviation and Radio Service would visit the church. The church needed volunteers to provide a meal. The teacher finished his appeal by saying, "We really need some volunteers to cook and serve those people in JARS."

My parents immediately sank behind their Bibles, struggling for control.

Another time my sister endured what must have been the most uncomfortable prayer service of her life. She heard a young man with the most nasal tone of voice she'd ever heard lay out a string of requests addressed to the Almighty with an incredible number of "eths" added.

"Dear Father," he intoned. "Blesseth Thoueth thiseth meeting hereeth in Thy presence." Giggles bubbled up inside Becky like a newly opened bottle of ginger ale, threatening to burst from her mouth and nose. She instinctively cupped her mouth with one hand and her nose with the other. This action resulted in an emission that sounded like a suckling pig. Then there was a blessed pause. *Whew, perhaps I'm saved!* She thought. But no. He began again, "And ifeth it pleaseth Thou. . ."

At this point my poor sister began to wheeze. It was the prayereth that hadeth no endeth.

Most of us who have attended church over a lifetime have a story to tell about bloopers spotted in a church bulletin. Someone passed the following jewels to me via cyberspace:

- *This morning's sermon is entitled "Jesus Walks on Water." This evening's sermon is entitled, "Searching for Jesus."*
- *Please place your donation in the envelope*

along with the deceased person you want remembered.

- *This evening at 7:00 p.m. come join in our 10th Annual Hymn Sing. Come prepared to sin!*
- *The Associate Minister unveiled our new tithing campaign slogan last Sunday: "I Upped MY Pledge. Up YOURS!"*

The scriptures indicate that a merry heart is good medicine. With all the stress in the world, perhaps that's one reason God doesn't let the faithful take themselves too seriously for too long! Meanwhile, keep those tissues ready to fake a good cry or sneeze if you land in the unenviable position of being the Lone Laugher.

Eye hath not seen, nor ear heard, neither have entered into the heart of man, the things which God hath prepared for them that love him.
1 CORINTHIANS 2:9 KJV

Chapter 24

Life in the Slow Lane

Ten years ago my friend Laura and I forsook city life and headed to the country. Weary from our overscheduled routines, we decided to rent a car and let the day unfold like the highway before us. If we weren't sure which road to take we could always lick our pointer fingers, roll down the windows, and go with the direction of the wind. We hit the road and before long, we entered a tiny town not far from Franklin, Tennessee, called Lieper's Fork.

We took in the town with one glance. The Country Boy Diner was on the left side of town and Bi-Rite convenience store was on the right. We noted with curiosity a sign at Hillsborough Road and a cross street. The stop sign had a smaller sign attached just beneath it that read, "Hillsborough Road Does Not Stop."

Laura and I did a simultaneous double take and chimed, *"Ever?"* It was the first time I'd seen a sign like that so I facetiously said, "Hey, I've always wanted to go to China. I guess if we stay on Hillsborough Road and head west. . ."

Later we walked into the Country Boy Diner and stepped back in time. An old-timey soda fountain was surrounded by Pepto-Bismal-pink swivel stools. Wood-paneled walls and well-worn booths provided a homespun hangout. The cracks and indentions in the seats revealed that apparently locals spent many hours lingering over fresh coffee and homemade pies. I moseyed over to a small bulletin board near the restrooms and was surprised to see autographed photos of country singers who had frequented the diner.

Then I noticed a larger board prominently displayed at the front of the store. It was crammed with photos of gap-toothed grandchildren, announcements of choir performances at the local Baptist church, and newspaper clippings about the town pride—the little league baseball team. This struck me as a little odd. Where I come from, the photos of stars would have been center stage, family photos tucked out of sight in wallets, and community events buried somewhere in the newspaper.

I noticed old farmers with weather-wrinkled

faces, middle-aged ladies with tightly permed "do's" and pretty young cowgirls wearing jeans and little makeup. But what struck me most was this: *Everyone seemed at home, and no one appeared to be in a hurry.*

As I wandered back to my booth where Laura was waiting along with my blue plate special (meatloaf and mashed potatoes—um, good), I said, "Boy, I kind of envy this one-restaurant town. The pace of life seems so laid-back and carefree."

"No kiddin'," Laura agreed, "it's a nice change from the chaos and pretense back in the city."

In an era in which we can pick up the dry cleaning, gas up the car, and wolf down a burger without the seat of our pants ever leaving the driver's seat, it's nice to be reminded that things weren't always so convenient. . .or impersonal. I don't think we've done ourselves any favors by dispensing with local watering holes where we could count on seeing familiar faces and catching up on each others' lives over coffee and cobbler. But we can still make a point to slow down and "sit a spell"—whether on a front porch swing or at a kitchen table—and enjoy a slice of our suburbanized version of small-town Americana.

Remember the days of old; consider the generations long past. Ask your father and he will tell you, your elders, and they will explain to you.
Deuteronomy 32:7

Chapter 25

Star Gazin'

One afternoon, ten years ago, my sister, Becky, invited me to join her on a business trip to Nashville. I was then a town-bound mother of one busy little boy, and the thought of being sprung sans son had me flying high with anticipation.

Once we were settled into our B&B, Becky and I sat at the fireside, sipping cocoa. "Are we livin' or what?" Becky said, grinning. "Whatcha wanna do tomorrow?"

"Well, I can't leave Nashville without seeing at least one star," I answered, then added confidently, "Where there's a will, there's a way!"

Becky choked on her cocoa, and her countenance changed from upbeat to playfully suspicious (knowing her little sister could be a smidgen too unconventional for her comfort zone at times). Clearing her throat she ventured, "What exactly do you have in mind?"

"Oh, nothing in particular," I falsely reassured, flashing a mischievous smile. "Not to worry."

Later that night at Finezza Italian Tratoria, between bites of polenta topped with carmelized onion, I asked our waiter, "Do you know the best place around here to see a country star?"

Amused by my candidness (or hickness, as Becky later teased), he replied, "You might see someone at Kroger. Even stars need groceries." *Now we're getting somewhere,* I thought with visions of coming eyeball to eyeball with Garth and Trisha over kiwi and kumquats.

Off to Kroger we went. While Becky kept her distance, I milled around the produce section. After half an hour, it was clear that the stars were not out that night. I hung my head in defeat and bought a chocolate bar and diet soda to drown my disappointment.

The next day, out on the town again, we made a pit stop at McDonald's. A teenage girl took my order. I couldn't resist asking, "I see you have a nice playland. Does Naomi ever bring Wynonna's kid here to play?"

The teen looked at me as if to say, "There's one born every minute," but responded politely, "Um. . .

No, ma'am. I've never seen the Judds at our play-land."

"Give it up, Rach," Becky teased, poking me in my McRibs. . .I mean, ribs. "Have you no shame?"

Maybe she has a point, I tried to reason silently with my unreasonable self. *I don't want to miss out on other fun stuff to do and see by being so bent on spotting a country music star.*

So I decided to put my star-struck agenda on the back burner and go along for the ride—wherever it might take me. Becky had several free hours before a meeting, so we motored away from the Golden Arches and headed to the back hills. As a young mom starved for uninterrupted conversation with an adult, I chatted my little ol' head off and had a grand time reconnecting with my big sister.

Later that night, Becky and I debriefed our B&B hostess about our day's travels and how much fun we had just being together, talking and laughing. The hostess replied, "Wow, you guys were right in Judd territory. Did you see their houses?"

My smile vanished, and I stuttered, "Wha–aa–at do you mean?"

"Well, that big gated white house with columns you mentioned seeing is Naomi's place. The cottage just down the road from there on the right is Ashley's place. And Wynonna lives just down from her," our hostess explained.

We use an expression in Texas that was very

appropriate for this situation: *Well, shut my mouth!* Boy, I wish somebody had shut *my* mouth while roaming those back hills with Becky. If we had only made a couple of pit stops in them thar hills and asked a few questions, we just might have seen some stars, or at least *known* we were driving by their homes!

Oh well, sometimes it pays to put our agenda aside, and sometimes it pays to hang on just a little longer. To quote the back end of a famous prayer, "May God grant us the wisdom to know the difference."

Delight yourself in the LORD and he will give you the desires of your heart.
PSALM 37:4

Chapter 26

Ding Dong! Perfectionist Calling

One freelance editor, who keeps me from swerving too far from literary propriety, is Lynn Marie, a strict (but very nice!) grammarian with a preference for perfection. Lynn Marie just loves words *and* the rules governing their usage.

And me? Or rather, I?

I'm more of an off-the-top-of-my-head writer. I contend that writing creatively and humorously is more art than science, and that's why I look more like Mona Lisa than Carl Sagan. But actually, I need both—art *and* science—to make my writing "work"—at least well enough for someone to pay me for it!

Since I'm a hang loose sort of writer, my brain

doesn't freeze up at the prospect of filling a blank page, as so many writers experience. Where my mind *does* freeze up is when I have to go over and over and *over* my "art." Therefore, I need to add a good measure of "science" (the proper use of language) to make my writing worth something to my readers.

Can you see now why I need Lynn Marie? We have wrangled over a few words and usages over the years while working together. One of our favorite tugs-of-war was over the name spelling of the delectable, cream-filled chocolate snack cakes called Ding Dongs. I had used the word in a vignette and without a hyphen.

Ever-vigilant Lynn Marie noticed the blank space where she believed a hyphen should be and began her search for accuracy. At the time, her husband had recently recovered from heart surgery so there were certainly no Ding Dongs in her cupboards. And we needed the information in a hurry. Providentially Lynn Marie's husband happened to be at the grocery store, so she dialed his cell phone and was relieved that Mike picked up the call:

"Whew! Sweetie, I'm so glad you answered," Lynn Marie began.

"No problem. Did you forget something?"

"No, not me. I think Rachel forgot something, and you know what a stickler I am when it comes to grammar."

"Uh-huh," Michael replied, eyeing the tofu section, his head swimming with the prospect of all the "meat" now made from soybeans.

"Well," Lynn Marie breezed on, "I need to know if Ding Dongs are hyphenated. Can you go look at a package and put me out of my misery, er, settle the mystery."

"For goodness' sake, honey," Mike responded, half-listening, "Of course they're hydrogenated. You know we can't eat that junk anymore."

Lynn Marie and I shared a good laugh over that story more than once! In fact, we had a friendly verbal tussle over who owned rights to this story that we were both certain would skyrocket one of our careers to the moon. (Oooh, speaking of the moon and snack cakes, have you tried a Moon Pie? Two graham crackers filled with marshmallow and dipped in chocolate—simply heaven.)

Alas, my friend-editor agreed to let me have the snack cake story, and eat one, too—with her tongue-in-cheek blessing for hydrogenated arteries.

In case you're wondering, our research revealed that, depending upon the circumstances, Ding Dongs, the snack cake, are not hyphenated. In other cases, the words may or may not be hyphenated depending on the usage and the publisher's preference.

If you have a tendency to want things "just so,"

you may relate to my friend's drive to know *the* answer. But you may also have learned at times it's okay not to have a definitive answer when one doesn't exist or is too complicated or time-consuming to unearth. And you may have also become more comfortable with the idea that there could be more than one approach to some things.

It's good to be flexible now and then. Like right now. I can't decide if I'd rather eat a Ding Dong or a Moon Pie. I'm pretty sure this is one of those situations in which there's not one right answer.

If any of you lacks wisdom, he should ask God,
who gives generously to all without finding fault,
and it will be given to him.
JAMES 1:5

Chapter 27

Grace Folks

I have a confession to make: I don't like mean people.

I'm not speaking of overtly mean people, but the covert kind—those who put on a happy face and *masquerade* as nice people, making it hard to see them coming. The folks I'm referring to seem to actually enjoy making others feel small by insinuating that they don't measure up to certain standards.

When they walk into a room, they bring with them a palpable tension. Any hope of relaxing and being yourself evaporates like water on a frying pan. You can kiss swinging on the chandelier good-bye, for sure.

Do you know people like this? Folks who seem to be the embodiment of what the scriptures refer to as "the law"—the practice of keeping Old Testament laws and performing certain rituals in order to be acceptable to God. But Jesus knew that when it came to transforming hearts, the law would fail miserably. Only grace could save the day—and all of humanity with it.

Law Folks usually feel a need to control people and situations. Conversely, Grace Folks are at ease with themselves and others. Typically, they have been humbled through a painful life experience in which they realized their deep need for God. As for controlling things—they've given up completely, letting God call the shots.

We love to be around Grace Folks. They're like the Grandpas who give us candy behind Grandma's back. They don't mind bending rules now and then for the sake of relationships. We can relax in their presence. They love us and accept us right where we are. Grace People give us not only the room to grow, but also the *motivation* to grow—at our own pace, in our own way.

Additionally, Grace Folks are "comfortable in their own skin"—they've given up pleasing people and have taken up pleasing God. As a result, they live more in line with their own God-given desires and personality style. Interestingly, this "getting comfy in your skin" phenomenon usually takes place later in life—at a time when your real skin is beginning to do funky things. It begins creasing, wrinkling, rolling, and even *hanging*. It's like your epidermis transforms into a walking Cirque du Soleil—performing feats that seem unnatural, and even freakish.

But who really cares about aging exteriors? When you're comfortable with who you are and put others at ease in your presence, no one really gives a flip how you look. What matters most is your magnetic interior (something vaguely reminiscent of a charismatic carpenter of Middle Eastern origin).

If you catch yourself getting bent out of shape lately, perhaps you've been trying to stuff yourself into the wrong mold and trying to live up to the standards that someone has defined for you. Forcing yourself into others' molds will only breed resentment. In the end, our lives should conform to the shape that God designed.

Your beauty should not come from outward
adornment. . .it should be that of your inner self,
the unfading beauty of a gentle and quiet spirit,
which is of great worth in God's sight.
1 PETER 3:3–4

Chapter 28

Happy Talk

My parents really enjoy each other's company—
they always have, ever since hooking up as high
school sweethearts. They insist one of the secrets
to a great relationship is communication. As Mom
puts it, "Happy couples chitchat. They banter. They
have repartee. Not just the girls. The guys, too!"

Her words reminded me of the song "Happy
Talk," sung by the character Bloody Mary to two
young lovers in the musical, *South Pacific*. In the
first few lines of singing, she encourages them to
talk about what they like to do and points out that
if they don't have dreams, they can't make their
dreams come true.

Maybe that simple song has a profound message

for today's busy couples. My parents, who are in their late sixties, have always been good at small talk as well as "deep" talk. It takes both kinds to keep the heart fires stoked.

My mother loves words and engaging conversation. My dad is a former aerospace engineer who also enjoys stimulating verbal exchange. In fact, his happiest moments since retirement are when he loads Mom into his pickup truck (in the front cab, in case you were wondering) and heads for the Texas hill country—enjoying a leisurely ride and spontaneous rhetoric with his sweetie.

On one particularly gorgeous day, Mom and Dad were making their Saturday afternoon drive to Glen Rose, Texas, admiring the rose bushes in bloom along the way. I wouldn't normally say that Mom has a habit of running off at the mouth, but this day she was especially talkative. She kept up a good while until she noticed that her usually good-natured partner wasn't responding much.

"I just love chitchat, don't you, honey?" She tried to entice Dad into the one-sided conversation, knowing that men need to talk, too, even if they need a little prodding. "There's a lot to be said for chitchat, I always say," she ventured again.

Dad turned to her slowly, peered over his glasses, and quietly answered with a smile, "Yes, dear. But there's a difference between chitchat and *drivel*."

On another day when she had forgotten an

important appointment, he asked her why she didn't write things on her calendar—*and* check it now and then.

"I don't know why you would question anything I do," she replied with tongue in cheek, "as being less than carefully thought out and *precisely* executed." Once again, his glasses slipped down on his nose as he fixed her with his gaze.

"This," he said deliberately, "from the Queen of Wing It?"

She wins a few; he wins a few more. But the important thing is they relish playing this good-natured game of gab together every day, *throughout* the day. It only draws them closer—further cementing their already adoring affection for each other.

So at least one secret to a good marriage, as attested to by my parents (and a Polynesian matchmaker!), is to develop a capacity for chitchat, banter, and repartee. Not sure what the difference is between all these? I wasn't either. Here are a few definitions to clear up any conversational confusion. May you and your guy enjoy some Happy Talk of your own—but God forbid you let it degenerate into drivel!

Chitchat: casual conversation; small talk
Banter: good humored, playful conversation
Repartee: a swift, witty reply; a ready or spirited retort
Drivel: to talk stupidly or childishly

And it came to pass. . .that Abimelech. . .
looked out at a window, and saw. . .Isaac
was sporting with Rebekah his wife.
GENESIS 26:8 KJV

Chapter 29

Death-Wish Fish

After nine months of formally writing my ideas for a new book I wanted to present to a publisher, I finally collapsed over the finish line on the oddly appropriate day of Halloween. Earlier in the day, my agent's partner, Julie, and I had exchanged e-mails at a fast and furious pace (no doubt she was concerned I might not finish if not cheered to the end).

Earlier that morning, I had thought of Julie in a complimentary, but concerning way while researching the Web site of celebrated singer-songwriter Rich Mullins ("Sing Your Praise to the Lord"). It had seemed to me that a number of Christians like Rich Mullins and Brent Curtis, coauthor of *The Sacred Romance*, proponents of "radical grace," seemed to get their tickets to heaven a little early. Both men died at fairly young ages.

So I wrote a cautionary e-mail:

> *Julie,*
>
> *After reading about Rich and Brent, I forbid you from being a student of radical grace or whatever it is that makes the really good Christians suddenly disappear. Okay?*
>
> *P.S. How about I send you some nice books on legalism and judgment?*

Julie's response:

> *Rach,*
>
> *You must be GIDDY about having this proposal done. Don't worry. I sin plenty enough to keep the scales balanced. I don't think I'll be disappearing any time soon.*

Good. That was settled then.

Later that afternoon I wrote Julie another e-mail in which I included last-minute edits for one of the chapters of the book. The excerpt read:

> *There has been what appears at first glance to be a benign culinary phenomenon taking place in this country. For hundreds, perhaps*

thousands of years, our palates have come to know and love fish with respectable one and two syllable names like trout, bass, catfish, and tuna.

But lately, it seems we've tossed aside any hint of species loyalty and have rushed head-long into the fins of a fish with a four-syllable name that sounds like an exotic dancer. Yes, I'm referring to the new white meat destined to put Charlie the Tuna out of business. The one, the only: tilapia.

Has anyone asked where this fish has been all our lives?

At chapter's end, I jokingly conclude that per-haps there's a plot afoot by some ill-meaning fish-mongers to do us in—one piece of fish at a time. After hitting SEND I took a break and went out to dinner. Later, I checked in with Julie again.

Julie,

I went to a restaurant tonight that had a new featured dish: jalapeño garlic tilapia.

I was thinking, I hope we get a taker on this book in time to capitalize on this fish frenzy. Anyway, it was delicious. I hope it was poisoned.

As is my hasty bad habit, I reread my e-mail *after* hitting SEND and, to my horror, realized that I had typed "was" poisoned instead of "wasn't."

The retraction e-mail:

> *Julie,*
> *I meant to write, "WASN'T poisoned." You're going to get us both killed (either by radical grace or tainted tilapia).*

Isn't it amazing how easy it is to miscommunicate? In the space of seconds, my e-mail exchanges had taken on the aura of that "gossip" game where you sit in a circle and whisper a sentence, only to find at the end of the game that the sentence bears no resemblance to the original one uttered.

Fortunately, in this case no real harm was done, but I have learned the hard way that e-mail is best saved for "all things positive and mundane." What to do with the other kind of communication? Pick up the phone or meet face-to-face. Better safe than sorry. . .or insinuating your early demise by virtue of the wrong verb tense.

> *Let your conversation be always full of grace,*
> *seasoned with salt, so that you may*
> *know how to answer everyone.*
> COLOSSIANS 4:6

Chapter 30

Sizzling After Sixty

As I enter my forties and notice more wrinkles and bulges from head to toe, I have become more curious about the "birds and bees" in a person's advancing years. The other day I saw a book titled *Sex After Sixty*. Glancing around to make sure my pastor wasn't in the bookstore, I casually picked it up and flipped through the pages. The contents shocked me. Every page was filled with nothing but. . .white space.

A few days later, I dropped by my mom's house. When I told her about falling for the book, she laughed.

"Don't you believe it!" she assured me. "There's plenty of adventure to fill that book, for the *fun* of it, if nothing else. I remember the card your dad received from a buddy for his sixtieth birthday. The front pointed out that at our age, sex isn't exactly the Fourth of July. Inside the card, it said at our age sex is more like Thanksgiving."

Mom continued, "To adjust to the changes that come along with the wrinkles and pounds. . ." (*Now we're getting somewhere,* I thought.) ". . . you gotta learn to laugh. One winter's night, my Sweet Thang hopped into bed before I did. When I joined him, I squealed with ecstatic gratitude. He had remembered to turn on my side of the electric blanket!"

Well, now I was laughing, but feeling a smidgen sorry for the old folks when Mom explained, "Have you ever heard the lines from Robert Browning's poem? 'Grow old along with me! The best is yet to be'?"

"Sure," I said, nodding. "But the motto for most of my generation is more like 'Grow to midlife with me, then let's divorce.'"

Mom chuckled and said, "Yes, I'm not sure what to make of your generation! But I wouldn't trade any part of our marriage of fifty years for the part we're in right now—not even the years when I was in my prime and you and your siblings made our rendezvous a lot more challenging!

"Then came our Empty Nest phase. For most couples, if things go as planned, the kids all grow up and go away, and Mom and Dad are alone again. By this time, the soil of understanding, affection, and experience has been tilled. The hormones are still pumping well, and Cupid finds he has a couple of pros to work with.

"But as time goes by, Aunt Minnie Paws drops in to visit Mom about the same time Dad finds that his Don-Juan Readiness can't always be counted on. Add to that a natural drop in energy levels, and you may well have to take a nap before enjoying a nighttime romance."

"So much for spontaneity!" I quipped.

"Well, sometimes, yes, spontaneity goes out the window. However, when love has been growing as it should, Mom and Dad find that they *like* each other so much more than when they were first married. By this time, deep affection has usually replaced less reliable passion. Tender understanding of the physical changes each has experienced can lead over-sixty couples to explore new ways of expressing the joy of coming together.

"Next day, Don Juan struts off to the golf course with a spring in his step and a glint in his eye. Mom can hardly remember how it feels to be sixty-five, now that she's sixteen again."

Pausing for breath, Mom winked at me and advised, "Take your vitamins—there's definitely sex after sixty! Rarely do the pages of a good, long marriage go blank until well past that age."

In our culture of "instant" everything—from microwave meals to spray-on suntans, we can lose sight of the concept that many things get better with time. Wine and cheese for example. Kids, too (although some of you will beg to differ). And according to long-timers, intimacy in marriage also gets better over time if you have two people who are willing to "grow the distance" with each other.

> *Therefore shall a man leave his father*
> *and his mother, and shall cleave unto*
> *his wife: and they shall be one flesh.*
> GENESIS 2:24 KJV

Chapter 31

By the Book

Let's talk about the corporate world, shall we? I know little about it personally, but I've heard quite a bit from my dad. He has thirty years of experience in the aerospace industry with its endless government red tape and rules. People who work in that kind of atmosphere tend to develop survival skills and often manage to really enjoy their jobs.

Now and then in my dad's workplace, some unidentified maverick employee would occasionally write an anonymous piece, spoofing one thing or another in their by-the-book work world. Then the piece would mysteriously appear on someone's desk. That tense recipient, under extreme duress and a deadline, no doubt, would glance at the paper, glance again, drop his pencil, look closely at the paper, and suddenly laugh out loud.

"Hey!" he would call to the person at the next desk, "Look at this!" And off the piece would go on its rounds, brightening everybody's day. Dad brought the following masterpiece home from work when I was in high school, and the whole family gathered round while he read it out loud, pausing now and then to recover from giggles.

Restroom Trip Policy

Effective today a new Restroom Trip Policy (RTP) will be established. Each month, employees will be given twenty Restroom Trip Credits (RTCs). The entrances to all restrooms will be equipped with voice recognition devices. Each employee must provide two copies of voiceprints (one normal, one under stress) to HR. If an employee's credits reach zero, the doors to the restroom will not unlock for that employee's voice until the first of the next month.

In addition, all stalls will be equipped with timed paper roll retractors. If the stall is occupied for more than three minutes, an alarm will sound. Thirty seconds after the alarm sounds, the roll of paper will retract, the toilet will flush, and the door will open.

The RTP is necessary to cut down on

dilly-dallying in the restrooms. Thank you in advance for your cooperation.

Clearly someone had had enough "by the book-ness" and was, in his own very maverick and funny way, saying, "Lighten up, will ya!"

Dad confirmed to us that yes, rigidity was often a problem in his workplace, but he was also mighty glad to have a good job among people with a great sense of humor. He gives attention to details, but God has also given him a deep appreciation of his fellow man that makes him a joy to be around. As skilled as Dad is with accuracy and adhering to rules, he would never put those things above showing his care for another person. He also knows how to lighten up. He always left his work at the office, and when he was home, he was ours to enjoy. He's a man who knows how to live by *the* book—the Good Book.

At times it's good to take personal inventory to see if we're really enjoying our lives and bringing joy to those we work with on the job or on a project or at home. Are these areas where you might need to "lighten up a little" with those around you?

May God help us remember that people are always more important than policy and that sometimes a little latitude and understanding will provide just the motivation someone else needs to get a job done—and done well.

Laugh Yourself to Sleep

A merry heart doeth good like a medicine:
but a broken spirit drieth the bones.
PROVERBS 17:22 KJV

Chapter 32

HGTV Junkie

Okay, be honest. How many of you are HGTV addicts? Count me in! I don't watch much television, but when I occasionally need company in the wee hours, there's no place like home—*Home and Garden Television*, that is.

One of my favorite programs is *Divine Design*. As soon as I hear the skat-style theme music (*dwee dow, a dat dat dwee dow...*) I come a runnin'. And could there possibly be a more beautiful, charming, multitalented host than Candice Olson? Don't you just love how she says in hushed, velvety tones, "*How...divine,*" when she presents the final room makeover?

Candice Olson is one of those women I would

like to hate, but she's too darn likeable. Even so, I enjoyed a small flashback to my angst-filled junior high school days the evening when I tuned into *Divine Design* and realized Candice was packing on some pounds.

"Yeah, I knew that stress would get to you, Candy! Couldn't stay away from the potato chips, huh? Welcome to the real world," I teased without mercy from my perch on the bed, nestled next to a box of vanilla wafers. Then I realized she was pregnant. Oh well, it's not her fault she's picture-perfect and camera ready.

When it comes to décor, Candice knows it all—from whimsical to traditional to dramatic, this chick knows her stuff—and struts it!

I've often wondered how Chico the Electric Man keeps from electrocuting himself, the way Candice sometimes flirts with him like a blushing schoolgirl. Other admirers and helpers include the painter who looks like a French artiste—small wonder he doesn't paint himself into a corner when Candice comes 'round in those tight jeans to check his work. And finally, there's the carpenter who looks like an All-American quarterback—he seems least affected by CO's alluring personality, but boy does he get smiley when she compliments his trim work!

Another favorite show of mine is *House Hunters* with Suzanne Wong. In each episode we are introduced to a couple wanting to buy a home, and the mission is accomplished without a hitch every time. So I find it quite humorous when Suzanne tries to build some drama before the commercial break to keep viewers tuned in. She usually says something like: "Will the Smiths choose the two-bedroom cottage with half bath that only accommodates half a person? Or will they pick the two-story colonial without stairs? Or perhaps the three-bedroom ranch that backs up to an emu farm? Coming up next on. . .*House Hunters*."

Designing for the Sexes is a program that features a couple whose tastes in decorating are opposite. For example, the man may be into big game hunting and the woman into floral arranging. The professional designer-host helps them meld the styles and compromise. So at show's end, you may see a stuffed raccoon clutching sprigs of dried lavender or a moose head encircled by a wildflower wreath. The couple usually says something like "You not only saved our family room, you saved our marriage!"

Sometimes I have to reach for the tissue box.

Finally, there's *Curb Appeal*. On this show a makeover team visits a couple whose house has a boring exterior appeal and wants to increase the "wow" factor. So the producers bring in a landscaper, carpenter, handyman, butcher, baker, and candlestick maker. Fifty-thousand bucks and a few topiaries later, the place is transformed into a quaint cottage suitable for the seven dwarfs—if only they could afford to live in the neighborhood.

I'm not certain why these makeover shows are so appealing, but I wonder if it has something to do with the fascinating process of seeing something transformed until it reaches its potential.

On a spiritual level, God is all about helping us realize our potential—our capacity for love in particular, as we love Him and others. In a real sense, our whole lives are about becoming conformed to the image of the Divine Designer. When we finally see Him face-to-face for *our* "reveal," it will be more thrilling than the most dramatic makeover we could ever see, even on HGTV.

Therefore, if anyone is in Christ,
he is a new creation; the old has gone,
the new has come! All this is from God.
2 CORINTHIANS 5:17–18

Chapter 33

The Secret Lives of Ops

The other day I realized I have an imaginary friend. Only it's not the kind of sweet, lovable companion you'd think I would conjure up to join me throughout the day.

She's no Laura Ingalls Wilder but instead is more like Nelly Olson. Remember her from the show *Little House on the Prairie*? Nelly was the blond, curly-haired daughter of the general store owner. And she was a Goody Two-Shoes who loved to tattle on the other kids, being careful to point out her finer points while exposing the less desirable ones of her playmates.

I call my unseen Nelly, "Other People" or OP for short. OP only comes out to play when I'm feeling lousy about myself. In "nana-nana-nana" tones I hear voices in my head, telling me how perfect OP is and what a loser I am.

For example, as I was grabbing my girls, football style under each arm, and rushing them headfirst into the van loudly lamenting, "We're going to be late to preschool! Get in your car seats and get buckled—*now*!" OP pops out to play with my head.

"I would never be so disorganized that the fruit of my ever-lovin' womb would be the last children to grace the doors of their classrooms. Children need time to transition, you know. Every good mother knows *that*."

With the tsk-tsking of OP's tongue still ringing in my ears, I lock the back door, slog to the van (laden with fairy-winged backpacks and Dora the Explorer lunchboxes), start the engine, and roar away. Halfway to school, I realize I'm barefoot, haven't combed my hair, and haven't applied one smidgen of makeup.

"Oh my," the voice begins again, "I would never embarrass *my* offspring by going out in public looking like I stepped out of the cave woman display at the Museum of Natural History."

The other day I finally realized that my imaginary nemesis-friend was just that—a figment of my imagination. And so I set out to write down all the rhetoric (aka "hooey") I've been filling my brain with from *The Secret Lives of Other People*:

OPs *rarely, if ever, raise their voices at their children ("Radcliffe, darling, you mustn't poke mummy in the eye.").*

OPs *never think ill of others. They are the embodiment of unconditional love.*

OPs *never get irritated, frustrated, or incarcerated.*

OPs *maintain immaculate, professionally decorated homes—even on a budget. After all, necessity is the mother of invention.*

OPs' *children have impeccable manners. They don't pick their noses—they pick up toys (and place them neatly in Pottery Barn designer bins).*

OPs *whistle while they work (never grumpy, always happy).*

OPs' *older children are excellent students, excel in athletics or arts, and spend their summers on mission trips.*

OPs *personally prepare the freshest, healthiest organic meals ("Salmon with dill sauce, anyone?").*

OPs *never miss a workout. They have a "core" and aren't afraid to use it.*

OPs *have a real knack for time management. They balance moneymaking, homemaking, childrearing, and lovemaking with ease—with time left over to cultivate their own interests.*

OPs *are immune to hormonal imbalances.*

They get eight hours of sleep and take "guaranteed absorption" vitamins.

OPs never miss morning meditation or get behind on their Beth Moore Bible studies.

OPs never feel even a twinge of envy regarding the cheerleader good looks, spiritual maturity, or "golden touch" blockbuster success of every venture Beth Moore sets her hand to.

When I wrote down my beliefs about "The Secret Lives of Other People," I realized how ludicrous and self-defeating these beliefs were. I've decided the next time I'm falling apart at the seams, I'll just say, "If you can't say anything nice, then don't say anything at all."

Do you compare yourself to an imaginary fiend, er. . .friend, too? Hey, nobody's perfect—even Other People. If we need to make some lifestyle changes, the more productive route is to find an older mentor who can take us through the paces. In the meantime, tell your imaginary friend to take a hike—and take her new Eddie Bauer hiking boots and down-filled vest with her.

For the accuser of our brothers, who accuses them before our God day and night, has been hurled down. They overcame him by the blood of the Lamb and by the word of their testimony.
REVELATION 12:10–11

Chapter 34

Who Turned Up the Heat?

One of the dearest privileges I reap from having written *Wake Up Laughing* is getting to know some of the readers via e-mail. I love that unconventional women of all age groups caught the offbeat messages and enjoyed some chuckles.

Since I like to write about topics that hit women where they live, as well as where they laugh, I asked a few over-fifty friends to write about the female version of global warming, or Aunt Minnie Paws, as my mom likes to refer to the change of life.

Let's begin with a little ditty about snuggling and sweat, shall we? I won't reveal its source to protect the not-so-innocent:

Laugh Yourself to Sleep

He wants to cuddle beneath warm *covers.*
For him it's January; for me—July hovers!
Has he not heard of spontaneous combustion?
The two of us—turned to ashes—
Not from passion, but rather hot flashes.

My mother was caught off guard by the approach of her Aunt Minnie Paws, feeling she would somehow remain forever young. With that misconception, she decided her electric blanket had gone completely haywire. One minute it was setting her on fire and the next, freezing her to death. One night when she couldn't get either her blanket or her box fan adjusted, frustrated from "thermostat confusion," she threw the fan into the wall, waking Dad out of a sound sleep. His hair suddenly turned near-white. Male Menopause, I guess.

The famous fan-toss incident was so out of character for Mom that the light finally began to dawn. That which had happened to her *old* mother was now, incredibly, happening to her. *Why is the onset of menopause such a surprise?* she wondered.

A trip to the gynecologist settled the issue, and she left his office clutching her estrogen and progesterone prescriptions and feeling a glimmer of hope. (These prescriptions are no longer recommended for our generation of Blazers, leaving us to our own innovative devices. Soy shake or black cohosh, anyone?) And sure 'nuff, with the passing of time, life got better for thermostat-challenged Mom. The sun began to shine more reliably, she made it over the hot hump, and, finally, over Menopause Mountain in one peaceful piece.

I watch Mom now with a twinge of what is *almost* envy. She flits about feeling fairly pleasant *all* month long. She and Dad seem to have even more sparkle in their shared smiles than before Mom's Big Change. He has apparently recovered from seeing their box fan heaved at their bedroom wall by a small, sweaty, fire-breathing woman. He was also smart enough to buy a dual-controlled electric blanket, with his-and-hers remotes!

A friend shared her take on The Change: "I've gone through lots of stages and changes in life. Each *ultimately* had its blessings—including menopause! I have turned a corner when it comes to how I view change. I used to think it was a disruptive fact of life, but now I realize that accepting it and realizing its possibilities depends on my attitude."

I can think of menopause as an unwelcome guest or as a chance to banish that pain-in-the-neck monthly visitor. I can dread those expected hot flashes or look forward to owning my very own dual-controlled electric blanket. Above all, I need to remember to hold tightly to my Master's hand through every change. Because He always remains the same, I can face my life's changes with confidence.

*Jesus Christ is the same yesterday
and today and forever.*
HEBREWS 13:8

Chapter 35

Cancer Shmancer!

Breast cancer has become so common that it seems almost epidemic. My mom's "Nature Man" gynecologist blames it on the proliferation of hormones in our air, food, and almost everything else that surrounds us. Others contend the toxins released into the air we breathe through industrial and chemical waste cause it. Whatever the source, I remember a pithy saying I used to hear from my grandmother's sweet, nonsensical mouth, " 'Tain't funny, McGee!"

So now we're told we shouldn't take hormone pills anymore, which leaves us with the prospect of cold turkey menopause—alternately sweltering and shivering through our nights. No matter.

Hormone-free menopause leaves lots of women wandering through the house most nights any-way—wide-awake from 4:00 a.m. 'til breakfast! In the meantime, let's pray that this recent edict from the Top Medical Brains in the Land will slow down the occurrence of this dreaded disease.

Some of the bravest women I know have cried, laughed, and prayed their way through breast cancer. Among the bravest is Doylene Gilliland, who e-mailed me about her experience after reading *Wake Up Laughing*:

> *In August of 2000, at the age of forty-two, I was diagnosed with breast cancer. Faith and humor got me through the darkest days and insomniac nights. For instance, losing my hair was not as traumatic for me as it was for my husband. When I came home from my first chemotherapy treatment, we talked about the implications of my new reality, and he asked if I would lose my hair.*
>
> *"Yes." I decided not to sugarcoat the news. "Most of it will be gone before my next treat-ment in three weeks."*
>
> *"Gee." He grinned. "I hadn't planned on being married to someone who's bald."*
>
> *"Ha!" I shot back, "Neither had I!"*
>
> *So we discovered right away how much humor helps when you're hurting. And my*

hurting had just gotten started! After I fin-
ished chemo and radiation and thought I was
home free, I decided to have saline implants to
replace the real thing. What was I thinking?
I ended up with staph infections twice and a
strep infection. I've had a wound-vac the size
of a car battery attached to my chest by way of a
suction hose. I've had two rolls of Kurlex gauze
(thirteen feet each) pushed inch by inch into my
open wound.

I've been poked, prodded, and punctured
by the best of 'em. But the most valuable thing
I've learned out of all of this is that God is so
good! On the day of my diagnosis, I promised
Him I would glorify Him through it all, and
He rewarded me with marvelous moments
of humor to soothe my aching body and soul.
For example, have you ever seen a bald lady
with Bubba teeth? I met her in my mirror one
morning, and take it from me, it's hysterical!

Furthermore, I've learned that, for me at
least, breasts have been highly overrated. I
can now put mine in the dresser drawer for
the night and sleep on my stomach. I haven't
enjoyed that luxury since I was ten! Now I'm
waiting until I can take my teeth out at night,
too!

I tell other women that if you're dealing
with a calamitous event, trust in God's love.

*Don't camp out in the "valley of the shadow"—
remember, we are only passing through!*

I'm humbled by correspondence from readers like Doylene. I am grateful for the wisdom these women lovingly bestow on me—teaching me in often wacky, vulnerable, and eloquent ways, that even when we don't understand, we can still trust God and rely on His love and care.

*And God shall wipe away all tears from their eyes;
and there shall be no more death, neither sorrow,
nor crying, neither shall there be any more pain:
for the former things are passed away.*
REVELATION 21:4 KJV

Chapter 36

Don't Throw Out the Baby

The other day I ran across an interesting bit of etymology about the phrase, "Don't throw the baby out with the bathwater." According to the source I was reading, the phrase referred to a time when bathwater was shared by an entire family, with the adults and children bathing first, and Baby bathing last. Obviously the water would turn increasingly murky, thus the phrase, "Don't throw the baby out with the bathwater."

I assume Baby was last because he was the least able to complain.

Today we use this quaint phrase to describe situations in which we may quit after trying to deal with a difficult situation, only realizing later that we also gave up some benefits that could have been ours, if we'd just exercised a little more patience.

For example, my marriage has often been the modern version of the classic sitcom, *The Odd Couple*. I'm Oscar (the disheveled disaster) and Scott is Felix (the neat freak). Scott has an uncanny gift for cleaning and de-cluttering almost any area—a closet, a junk drawer, my van, and the girls' art drawers.

When I get behind on keeping up with clutter, Scott often offers to help me. (I suspect his offer is not as selfless as it may appear on the surface. I think it's often more as if he's saying, "Help me help you help *me* get this junk out of my sight!")

With amazing speed, Scott can dump my Trash N Treasure (TNT, a rather apropos acronym) piles onto the floor and categorize the contents in smaller piles for my review. You would think I would be thrilled to have the help. And part of me is. But another part is afraid he may overlook something important in those piles and, well, toss the baby out with the bathwater (i.e., perhaps a check is stuck to a Starbucks receipt by a piece of wayward ABC gum (already been chewed).

So when Scott is past the point of no return and forages through my TNT, I try to muster the mental fortitude to dive in first, thereby protecting potential treasures from accidental annihilation. Once I've had my shot at the mounds, I let Scott experience the "high" of dumping three-fourths of the annoying monstrosity into the trash can.

Odd Couple marriage dynamics aside, I generally do well at tolerating personalities that differ from my own. For example, during my twenties, I survived working for two very exacting financial executives (and kept up the morale of the troops, er, *staff* with my witty persona).

Yes, I made it through the heat of daily battle with these tough guys for years (although *they* didn't look so hot after my tenure). Let's just say that if the business world had an award that was the equivalent of a Purple Heart, I would have had a fighting chance at nabbing one.

Believe me, many days I would have loved to walk out of the office and leave them lecturing about the nuances of paper clip designs (some apparently make indentations on documents—the horror!). Looking back, I'm glad I didn't. I would have missed not only their recommendation—which I needed to nab a better, less stressful position—but also some skills that later proved invaluable.

A wise mentor once told me, "I think that as we live, very few things are more important than developing patience." A popular caption often found on posters or greeting cards with a picture of a lion cub precariously clutching a tree limb advises, "Hangeth thou in there."

May we learn to hang in there when a challenging situation turns murky and our first instinct is to toss the baby out with the bathwater. In time, we'll probably be glad we showed restraint and developed a little more patience (that we can apply to the next challenge!).

But let patience have her perfect work,
that ye may be perfect and entire, wanting nothing.
JAMES 1:4 KJV

Chapter 37

Mother's Day "Out"

Recently my mother was having a terrible time forgetting things—from double booking a few social engagements to discovering things in the microwave she didn't remember putting in there. That's par for the course for me, so I wasn't sure what the big deal was. But Mom became so concerned about her noggin that she decided to have a look inside.

When the neurologist told Mother that she would need to have a closed MRI, Mom almost bolted from the office.

"I'm sorry, but I just don't *do* tight places," Mom insisted.

"You'll be fine. Just take this pill thirty minutes before and that should relax you," Dr. Hughes soothed, while placing a white pill the size of a Tic-Tac in Mother's sweaty palm.

On the morning of the test, Mom took the pill thirty minutes before her appointment. When she arrived at the lab with my father, the receptionist told them, "We're running about a half hour behind if you'd like to run an errand and come back."

My folks wandered to the charming coffee shop down the street. Mom sat at a round table embellished with yellow and red Mexican tile, while Dad went to fetch two cups of joe. As Dad walked back toward Mom, he saw that she was resting her head on the table—mouth open, eyes shut.

When Dad got within earshot, he called out, "Oh, good one, Ruthie. There's no way that pill knocked you out *that* fast!"

But alas, Sleeping Beauty Ruthie did not rise from her drug-induced stupor, and Prince George knew he had a royal situation on his hands. He asked the friendly barista to keep an eye on his passed-out princess while he went to fetch the carriage—a four horse-powered Oldsmobile sedan.

Dad got Mom back to the lab, but she soon began sliding out of her chair at regular intervals and landing in positions that were, well, unbecoming of a Sunday school teacher's wife.

"I'm sorry, Mr. Arnold, we are running an hour late now," Ms. Behind announced apologetically. Half-panicked, Dad gazed at his Babe in La-La

Land, just in time to see her sliding about like a slick swordfish again. To his relief, the nurses finally loaded Mom in a wheelchair and deposited her into the MRI.

Dad reports that Mom came to long enough to join him for chitchat over a Whopper at Burger King for lunch. Mom says she has no memory of the burger or anything else during her day out—*cold*—on the town. Some pill!

The results of these shenanigans. . .I mean. . . *tests*? Turns out, Mom is no head case. However, she might be battling a big head, upon learning the results of her very first IQ test. She's not telling the results, but she has a new confidence and she's become unusually smiley. But she still can't remember what's in the microwave when it beeps.

On some days life gets to be a bit too much, and I wish I could check out for the day! Wouldn't it be great to have a temporary memory loss and totally forget the hassles waiting for you to untangle at work or home?

Well, we might not get that luxury without a legitimate prescription for a knockout drug, but God gives us that luxury when it comes to forgetting our mistakes. In fact, the Bible teaches that once we confess and repent of our sins, God experiences *permanent* memory loss—just as if He'd been knocked out cold.

Eli thought she was drunk and said to her, "How long will you keep on getting drunk? Get rid of your wine." "Not so, my lord," Hannah replied.
1 SAMUEL 1:13–15

Chapter 38

Comfort Zone Ejectors

Life in a fallen world has a way of regularly catapulting us out of our comfort zones. Whether the cause of liftoff is as small as getting confused at the Starbucks counter (while busy commuters stack up behind us) or as large as discovering that a spouse has been unfaithful, we can suddenly land hopelessly suspended in the Stratosphere of Stress.

Remember the song "Wouldn't It Be Loverly," sung by Liza in her cockney accent in the musical *My Fair Lady*? I think how loverly it would be to respond to stressful situations in ways that keep my feet on the ground instead of blasting off into orbit. Although it's unrealistic to greet every difficulty with Professor Higgins's stoicism, we might have a shot at responding in ways that will keep us from royally falling off the deep end.

When my husband was laid off from work and we lost all the outward "stuff" that reveals a person's "station" in life, I learned some very hard but valuable lessons about navigating life's Comfort Zone Ejectors. I know many women understand even better than I do that necessity is the mother of invention when it comes to coping with difficult circumstances. The necessity to remain relatively sane and keep dinner on the table for my young family inspired me to "invent" what I call the "Traits of a Spiritually Savvy Woman."

I wish I could tell you that I keep these principles top of mind, but quite honestly, I need refresher courses weekly, and sometimes daily! Perhaps you'd like to read along, while I indulge in some remedial training:

Four Traits of the Spiritually Savvy Woman

1) She's a Walking Pituitary Gland. *She sees every challenge as an opportunity to grow rather than a nuisance to endure.*

2) She's Not Afraid to "Go a Few Rounds" with God. *She's willing to step into the boxing ring and prayerfully "spar" with God. She's unflinchingly candid, yet certain He will eventually answer her cries for help!*

3) She prefers The Today Show to Back to the Future. *She doesn't get sidelined by the "what ifs" of tomorrow or the "if onlys" of yesterday.*

4) She's a Palms Up Woman. *She holds challenges with an open hand before God, being careful not to elbow Him out of the picture.*

Okay, I think I've got it now. If only I can "keep it" while trying to work, fix PB&J sandwiches, and settle sisterly rivalry—all at the same time. Wish me luck (or better yet, pray) and send me an e-mail about *your* Comfort Zone Ejectors and how you manage your time of suspended animation—I'm all ears! Speaking of ears—even if good advice tends to go in one ear and right out the next—there's always remedial school.

The LORD had said to Abram, "Leave your country, your people and your father's household and go to the land I will show you."
GENESIS 12:1

Chapter 39

Dawg

I often hear from readers who love animals and tell me wonderful stories about lessons they learn from their pets. The following story is one of the more poignant and powerful ones. I asked its author, Stacy Gunderson of Bedford, Texas, if I could share it with you. She said, "Of course not!" quickly followed by "Just teasin'."

So here goes:

Dawg was a stray, a mixed-breed Schnauzer. My son was just two, but Dawg instinctively knew to handle him with care. He tolerated my daughter's affection, his low, muttering growls reminding her not to mess with him.

I became his mother. I've never seen a dog love a person so. He'd stand up on his hind legs and beg to be hugged. When I came down to his level, he pressed his muzzle into my neck and all but sniffed me up his nose. I soon felt guilty about this. As much as he adored me, he seemed to be a hoodlum at heart, making it hard for me to return his unwavering love.

As soon as we all left for the day, Dawg would jump to the kitchen counter and help himself. If he managed to access a bathroom, he shredded (and often ingested) the contents of the wastebasket. If we left him outside he promptly dug under the fence. So we yelled and threatened, banished him to his corner, tied him to the table—nothing corrected his delinquent behavior. He might be good for weeks, and then give in to his baser instincts. I was ready to change his name to Dirty Dawg.

After a particularly disgusting offense, leaving me with a gross, smelly mess, I banished him to the utility room. While he cowered in the corner, I towered over him, making him understand that what he had done was unforgivable, and that he would now be locked in this room every time we left the house. When I stopped for breath, I looked into Dawg's face and suddenly realized I wasn't alone with him. Though a personal relationship with God was new to me, I knew something unusual was happening: I suddenly saw in my mind images of my past unholy behavior that still lingered in the wake of my salvation.

When I really looked at my dog, his eyes afraid and miserable, I realized that I must look that way to the Father at times

"Oh Jesus," I often had whispered. "Help me. Forgive me." And over and over again, He did. In that moment with Dawg, I felt mercy wash over me so powerfully that I choked and started to cry. I repented of my bitter anger and asked the Lord for patience. I stroked Dawg and spoke sweetly to him. He stopped shaking and nestled against me. While I tended him, something changed in us both. With time, his fear of abandonment lessened and his hoodlum escapades lessened while I discovered what it felt like to be truly forgiven and forgiving. Dawg is a different animal today, and I'm a different person. We are both still works in progress.

Aren't we all? And thank God for the beasts and the children and the spouses and friends who hang in there with us, not holding our sins against us but helping us grow in their spirit of forgiveness.

For as high as the heavens are above the earth,
so great is his love for those who fear him;
as far as the east is from the west, so far has
he removed our transgressions from us.
PSALM 103:11–12

Chapter 40

Life's Little Ups and Downs

I could have written most of this book about my Crazy Cousin Jamie. Once my wide-eyed, tow-headed, willowy-legged, adventure-loving cousin grew to womanhood, life was still far from routine and dull. Actually, it's been, and continues to be, anything but that.

Jamie married and had four children—two boys and two girls. But then her marriage dissolved, leaving Jamie with a dilemma: She needed a job, but she didn't want to leave her children in day care. Casting about for options, she settled on a grand plan, very much suited to Jamie. She became a foster parent for two teenage girls with Down Syndrome, named Dolly and Roxie. They're not sisters, but they were good friends when they came to live with Jamie, and they've had a great time for the last several years in Jamie's unorthodox household.

Now are you counting Jamie's children? There are six of them, and their adventures would actually fill a larger book than this one, but let's just start with the day that her youngest fell from the top of the outside of an escalator in a Houston department store. The star of this show was five-year-old Martha Kate, a cool and collected doll baby with a fantastic lisp.

Jamie and her mom had decided to take their troupe of six young'uns shopping. Intrepid, courageous women, wouldn't you say? However, both Jamie and her mom had grown accustomed to keeping up with Jamie's troupe and went about their shopping as planned, keeping an eye out for any who broke ranks.

Martha Kate, ever the curious and adventurous one, sidled over to the escalator and stood outside watching it rise and disappear at the top of its run—a long way up. She then became interested in the lower steps and leaned over the railing to see a little better. She held on to the railing and raised herself a bit to get a better look, and the escalator continued to do what escalators do. Very quickly, Martha was past the point of no return.

When Jamie happened to glance in Martha's direction, her little girl was halfway up the escalator—hanging on to the outside rail. Jamie and her mom started in Martha's direction, knowing they couldn't possibly reach her before she would lose her hold. Higher and higher she rose, her grip slipping with each inch. When she could hold on no longer, she dropped.

Incredibly, a woman who was much closer to the escalator than Jamie or her mom, stepped under Martha Kate as she fell, and the two of them went down together. Martha landed safely on top of her rescuer, her dress up to her waist. Nonplussed, she looked coolly at the lady and said, "My undahweah is showing." Although the lady was a bit bruised and shaken, she couldn't help but laugh.

You can imagine the tears, the joy, the relief, the gratitude poured out on both Martha Kate and her rescuer. Paramedics came rushing in and after checking things out, pronounced both Martha and the woman in good shape. Even so, the event did make the evening newspaper.

The story of Martha Kate goes on, however. She is now fourteen years old, and is 5 feet 8 inches tall, willow thin with a face like an exquisite china doll. She's been modeling some, but remains as cool and collected as ever. She goes about her life in school and her out-of-the-ordinary household and has a wonderful time with her sister, foster sisters, two big brothers, and a host of cousins who gather together at every opportunity, making wonderful memories, and rehashing so many old ones—like the day Martha Kate rode the escalator at the big department store—sort of.

> *Sons are a heritage from the LORD,*
> *children a reward from him.*
> PSALM 127:3

Chapter 41

Coattails

It's a financial fact of the new millennium that many stay-at-home-wannabe women have no choice but to get a job, or consider a home-based way to supplement the dwindling family coffers.

When I faced that situation I looked around at my family and saw—writers. There was Mom, my sister, my aunt—all published authors. I knew from watching them and their publishing successes and defeats that I would need to keep my part-time day job as a secretary.

Even so, I kept the long-term goal in view—working from home in my candy-striped PJs and bunny slippers, with my laughing hyena coffee mug nestled next to a Krispy Kreme donut. Does it get any better than that? I think not.

The coattailing thing bothered me at first. I wanted to be a self-made woman, not a parasite feeding off of someone else's success, even if they were in my own family. Then I met my sister for coffee one morning, and she clued me in.

"Rachel," she began, flashing her Ms. Optimist smile, "Think about it. Lawyers tend to beget lawyers, doctors tend to beget doctors, and actors tend to beget actors. Why would it be any different for writers? It's in our genes!"

"Wow...maybe you have a point," I, Ms. Realist, answered pensively, taking her encouragement cautiously to heart.

She then added, "Besides, if you stink it won't matter if your name is Ernest*ine* Hemingway. Editors will toss you out like yesterday's pizza."

I laughed. Nervously. Inside I was thinking, *Yikes, I don't know if I'm ready to face leather-skinned, saber-toothed editors who can't wait to flood the pages of my writing with red ink.*

Days later, as I worked discontentedly at a secretarial job, I thought about my sister's words. *Maybe I could write, at least well enough to make as much as I do typing and answering phones part-time.*

So I latched on in my mind's eye to that picture of me in bunny slippers with donut in hand, working from home. Then I held on for dear life while I sent my stuff out to the red-ink-dripping, saber-toothed editors.

Turns out some of them had normal teeth. And good hearts. A few wrote notes that indicated I wrote well, even though they couldn't publish my submissions. A few others told me I was funny and encouraged me to keep looking for a writing niche. Still others sent form letters of rejection. Sister Sunshine didn't let me focus on that for long.

"See, Rachel, I told you!" she gushed as if I'd won the Pulitzer. "A busy editor would never take time to jot a note if you stunk!"

Eventually my first short article was published regionally in *Better Homes and Gardens* (yeah, *that* was sweet!). Later when my husband was laid off and we were broke, my sister offered me some humor editing work, and eventually a contact of hers offered work that helped pay the winter heating bills.

Ten years later, I had the privilege of writing a small quirky book and, thanks again to my sister *and* my writer-editor mother (as well as more than sixty thousand unconventional women who read it), I got to write this small quirky book. I've had a virtual magic carpet ride on the coattails, er, skirt tails, of female writers in my family.

Are you a stay-at-home-wannabe who is exploring avenues for a vocational niche? You may need to look no farther than the family gene pool and dive in. If you're like me and feel embarrassed about accepting help from someone who is in a position to offer it—don't be. If you have the right stuff, it won't matter who helped you make the connections, *you* still have to deliver the goods.

Whether it's a friend, a family member, or acquaintance who offers you a leg up, just be thankful that God has placed that person of influence in your path. It probably wasn't long ago that someone gave *that person* a much-needed leg up. So here's to coattails: hold on tight, do the hard work, and enjoy the ride!

Beloved, I wish above all things
that thou mayest prosper and be in health,
even as thy soul prospereth.
3 JOHN 1:2 KJV

Chapter 42

When God Blinks

Over a year ago, I was flipping through channels on the tube and noticed a petite blond woman in her fifties cohosting a talk show called *Living the Life*. She was bright-eyed and all smiles. She also had a gift for funny turns of phrase, often catching her more serious sidekicks off guard and sending me rolling. It turns out that Louise DuArt is a comedian and impressionist and performs regularly with the legendary Tim Conway and Harvey Korman.

I knew instinctively that she was one of "us"—that sect of society I refer to as "Women Who Laugh Easily"—and decided to contact her. I hoped an assistant might pass my message on to her and, hopefully, brighten her day. So I wrote:

Louise,

I write inspirational humor and wanted to thank you for bringing such energy and levity to Living the Life!

Have you talked Pat Robertson into letting you cohost The 700 Club—*perhaps in drag, as Woody Allen?*

Thanks again for helping Christian women realize that humor is a vital part of a vibrant faith. Are you working on any other projects?

In Him,
Rachel St. John-Gilbert

Imagine my surprise when I received a reply, not from a loyal assistant, but from the Funny Girl herself:

Rachel,

Thanks so much for your e-mail. It's always encouraging to hear from someone who understands that our heavenly Father has given us humor to touch people.

My husband Squire has written a book called When God Winks. *A few weeks ago Oprah held up his book on her show and said it was one of her favorites. That was a miraculous God wink for us!*

I'm working on a live show for the over-fifty audience. I can relate on so many levels. . .

menopause, mood swings (I have more mood swings than Count Basie), hot flashes, the need to take chances, be silly, and get in touch with our inner child. (I got in touch with my child and found out she was a thumb sucker when under stress.) I'm still writing, even though I have only one menopausal brain cell to work with.

I'm in Reno with Tim & Harvey and have to run to do a sound check. I hope I remember my act!

Blessings,
Louise

I checked Louise's Web site and discovered that the DuArt-Conway-Korman trio was headed to Texas. I bought tickets for my budding impressionist son and myself. I also bought Squire's *When God Winks.*

I loved the premise of the book: that "coincidence"—mysterious guideposts that cause us to meet certain people, propel us in new directions, and place us in situations we never anticipated—are in fact, God winking, nudging us along a path toward destinations designed especially for us.

As much as I love Conway and Korman, Louise stole the show with her impressions of celebrities like Barbara Walters, George Burns, Cher, Martha Stewart, Fran Drescher, and others. Her ability to transition into the exact mannerisms and voices of so many people was beyond belief—freakish really (in the best possible sense of the word!).

I still occasionally touch base with Squire and Louise, and although our touchpoint was brief (more like a God blink), they shared wise counsel with me regarding my writing career and fueled Trevor's passion to pursue his comedic craft. Both Trevor and I are farther along our "God designed paths" for having met this very talented, giving couple.

We should never underestimate the nuances of daily life that may well be a God wink, straight from heaven. The more we raise our consciousness about God's omnipresence, the more we will recognize the winks, hugs, and laughter of a loving Father.

While he was still a long way off, his father saw him and was filled with compassion for him; he ran to his son, threw his arms around him and kissed him.
LUKE 15:20

Chapter 43

The Close Pin

My parents just celebrated fifty years of marriage. My husband and I are poised to ring in twenty years together this fall. I have some friends who have been married a long time and others who have called it quits. Even those couples like my parents still admit: "It isn't as easy as it looks sometimes."

I don't know of one right formula for "the perfect marriage," but I firmly believe that the couples who retain their ability to have fun together tend to stick together.

Witness my good friends Mike and Lynn. They've been married for more than thirty years. Lynn adores words (written and spoken) and is highly creative, while Mike is a man of few words and likes to make things. Lynn calls him her Renaissance man. After so many years together, they still love to have fun with each other. I asked her if she would share with me a little snapshot of the playful glue that keeps them together:

In the good old days when Mike and I were newlyweds, and before we'd bought our first dryer, I used to hang the clothes on a line in the basement or outdoors, weather permitting.

One day, as I pinned one of Michael's shirts to the line, for good measure I attached an extra clothespin to his shirttail. This was not the kind of shirt that Mike tucked in so he didn't notice the pin and wore the shirt in public with the clothespin dangling behind.

Although he never mentioned his tale of woe to me, one day in a meeting at my office, I was approached by a high-powered business executive who asked, "Lose something?" as he handed me a clothespin he'd detached from the back of my suit coat.

Talk about embarrassing! Talk about revenge. . .

I decided to get Mike but good. He had just begun his dignified job as usher at our church, and one glorious Sunday morning, both he and the clothespin proceeded down the sanctuary aisle in front of God and the whole congregation.

Over the course of thirty years, that pin has made its way into many locations: my purse, his shoe, my bra, his underwear. It's all in fun, and we have actually taken to calling it our "close pin."

Too often couples hang each other out on the laundry line of life to dry and twist in the wind in full view of others. Mike and Lynn's clothespin fetish isn't meant to pull each other down. Their clothespin symbolizes to them an "affection attachment." Many of us can reap some wisdom from the ongoing clothespin prank. Yep, we're pinned to each other for better or worse, for life, so doesn't it just make sense that we focus on ways to attach to our mates? Isn't this the meaning of love as God sees it—marriage as a picture of God's "affection attachment" for us—unconditional and intended for a lifetime?

You have stolen my heart, my sister, my bride;
you have stolen my heart.
SONG OF SOLOMON 4:9

Chapter 44

Strange Bedfellows

When I was a young girl, I loved to sleep with my grandmother, Nonnie, in her tall feather bed, piled high with colorful handmade quilts to keep the west Texas winter chill at bay. I had two siblings and too many cousins to count, so I did not always get to be Nonnie's "bedfellow," as she liked to say. But I relished each chance I got.

I've since heard the expression, "They make strange bedfellows." I am fond of the phrase, which pronounces two folks so different that it seems preposterous for them ever to share a tall feather bed at granny's house.

This phrase came to mind recently as I mulled the contents of my pantry. I had replaced the bad, ugly foods with good ones but had not stopped to notice the contrasting ideologies represented by the box and bottle labels.

For example, I had bought a delicious cereal filled with toasted pecans and dried apricots, but I had failed to notice that the picture on the box was of a religious guru wearing a turban. My son asked, "Hey, Mom, where's that Osama Bin Laden cereal?"

I had to bite my tongue from wisecracking, "Right next to the Smart-Bomb Fruit Chews, sweetie."

Well, I haven't researched what organization my money went to support (so hold your e-mails!), but I did have a good laugh when I saw that cereal perched next to the Ezekiel Bread. The packaging boasts: "Made from a biblical recipe."

I laughed at the juxtaposition. I might as well have put the Ted Kennedy Peanut Butter next to the George W. Bush Rice Bread. Or the Louis Farakan Salsa next to the Joel Osteen Organic Popcorn. Or perhaps Oprah's Wheatless Oatmeal Cookies beside the Pat Robertson Soy Milk.

I guess most folks know a good thing when they see it, whether they're conservative or liberal in their social or religious views. Healthy, natural food is easy to spot and easy to love.

When I see the mental and emotional energy some Christians expend in "winning" souls, comparing their own good labels with non-Christians' bad labels, I wonder if what we need more is love. We find unbelievers, our fellow men, strange and they, us. But if we could compassionately show the love of Christ, maybe they'd know a good thing when they see it. Maybe they'd find *Jesus* easy to love.

Taste and see that the LORD is good.
PSALM 34:8

Chapter 45

Weight for Me

For years I noted, though with a sense of detachment, that many people over the age of forty joke about developing a "spare tire." Midsection weight never concerned me because I was born a "perfect pear"—you know, with hips and a waistline, but not much tummy. But that changed when I turned forty-two.

I would like to say that I didn't see it coming or do anything to cause it. But the truth is that I overate and under-exercised all that summer, and when it was time to come out of the pool and face the fall, I ended up with the equivalent of an inflatable swim ring permanently encircling my waist.

"How can this happen to me?" I asked the

plump stranger in my mirror. "I'm a *pear* for Pete's sake! How can I be an apple *and* a pear? I'm beginning to look like those guys in the Fruit of the Loom underwear commercials. What's next? A perfect pineapple?"

I tried reasoning with the middle-aged (yikes! I've said it!) smartie in the mirror.

"That little bitty swim ring isn't *that* noticeable. It's more like a smallish pork tenderloin round my middle." I set about to make the statement true by frantically searching in my closet for longer and fuller blouses. None of them was as cute as I'd remembered. Maybe I'd try something a little—well, younger. Off I went shopping and wouldn't you know, I soon noticed a woman about my age who was wearing a short-waisted, teeny-bopper top. The space between the bottom of her top and the top of her bottom looked like a giant muffin whose "batter" had oozed over the edges. Sighing, I turned back to the women's department.

There seemed to be only one way out, and you probably already know what it was: the much avoided diet and exercise plan. So, for the first time since I was a slightly chubby preteen and a card-carrying member of Weight Watchers, I enrolled in a weight-loss program. I had joined Weight Watchers so many times over the years they probably had a wing named after me at headquarters, but somehow I told myself this plan would be different. Gradually I'm learning to eat meals the "size of my loosely clenched fist" (chicken the size of my cell phone, salmon the size of my son's iPod) and chewing *tediously* slowly.

In weaker moments, I want to take my loosely clenched fist and wrap it, oh so lovingly, around a nice waffle cone filled with rocky-road ice cream smothered with hot fudge sauce and toasted pecans. Or I yearn for an eclair the size of my cell phone and iPod combined. At my detestable weakest, I'd like to wrap my tightly clinched fist around the instructor's neck and ask *tediously* slowly, "How would you like a breath of air the size of my fist?"

However, in my stronger moments, I'm learning real advantages in cutting my PB&J sandwich into four sections and chewing each bite like a cow chewing her cud, rather than stuffing it down while standing over the sink. The process is at least slowing down my intake, which helps me *look* less like a cow.

I've also realized that during my meals, I often stop and take the time to watch my little chicks playing happily in the sandbox, to notice the butterflies alighting on my red tulips, and other wonders of my surroundings. Hey! There are other things in life besides food! I missed these delights when I grazed at the speed of a wood-chipping machine.

Practically speaking, this slow-down technique

is designed to help my tummy tell my brain, "Excuse me, but I'm about to bust down here!" Theoretically this practice will keep me from tossing extra helpings down my gullet willy-nilly, thus deflating the built-in swim ring around my external middle.

Undoing a lifetime of unhealthy eating patterns is daunting and exhausting. Having to undo a lifetime of *anything* is exhausting. Some days I'm tempted to beat myself up and think *I'm such a loser...* or in this case such a *gainer*!

On other days, I'm encouraged that I'm learning a new way of being that might finally deflate my spare tire, jelly mold, floatie ring, love handles —whatever.

Yes, good things are happening. Somewhere between near starvation and grunts of agony during exercise, I learned that renewing my figure is very much tied to renewing my mind. Jesus loves me, this I know. I'm not alone in the battle of the bulge.

I can do everything through
him who gives me strength.
PHILIPPIANS 4:13

Chapter 46

Everyday Epiphanies

After the rush and chaos of the holiday season, I became distressed about the constant accumulation and reaccumulation of clutter and felt I was once again on the verge of a big life transition.

I had a pre-midlife crisis in my thirties, and now in my forties, I'm having a *near* midlife crisis. I'm trying hard not to have any more crises until I reach real midlife at age fifty and can finally, blessedly, call it a midlife crisis.

I like the term *epiphany* because it's a vivid word picture of an about-face. And I was a woman who needed some personal epiphanies that would enhance my everyday life and keep me from being cranky to live with.

I am also an "experience" person who enjoys a variety of visual and sensory practices such as listening to music, smelling the fragrance of candles, displaying fresh flowers, and creating niches in which to relax. The problem was, not much of this was happening, and the less it happened, the unhappier I became.

The bigger problem was that I knew I was going to write this book, and if my environment remained as it was, I would have to retitle the book, *Cry Yourself to Sleep—Offbeat Devotions for the Emotionally Unstable Woman*.

With the help of a life coach, I set out to "link beauty with the mundane" and enhance my daily experiences as a homemaker. For weeks I was outright manic about "creating order and beauty" in my home.

My tidy husband watched in disbelief as I transformed both the house and how I ran it before his bewildered, blinking eyes. After surveying our cottage-style food closet with its decorative wheat-colored baskets and vintage-looking handwritten labels, he said, "Now you're really scaring me. You're turning into *me*!"

I de-cluttered, set up systems for dealing with laundry and paperwork, rapped the knuckles of any family member who left junk on my kitchen counter, and created a few relaxing niches with comfy seating, small tables, and throw pillows.

I became the female counterpart to Dr. Phil,

constantly asking myself, "Is this working for me?" Often the answer was "no." And so the manic "Get 'er done, Rachel" got crackin' and began the mini-makeover of the space or room in question:

Loving that laundry!

I get overwhelmed with too much of anything, so now I only wash medium loads. Then I place them in soft-woven baskets that I enjoy touching so I'm more motivated to pick up the basket and deal with the small, clean load. I've made the laundry room more inviting with classical music pouring softly from a radio, whimsical pictures, candles, and lavender-scented hand lotion, detergent, and dryer sheets. If you gals buy enough copies of this book, I may get to put in black and white checkerboard tile—a look I've admired for years, but can't afford in a larger area. Talk it up, girls!

Clutter? What clutter?

I became a basket case and a hooker. I went crazy buying baskets and hooks. I once read about a professional decorator who swears by clutter catchers: baskets or other unique or eye-pleasing containers. Most clutter looks better in a basket, as long as it's not junk—magazines, photos, toys, CDs, for starters. As a stickler for details that will enhance my daily experiences,

I like soft, pliable baskets with leather or suede handles, since they don't hook on my clothes or break off pieces. And they just feel good in my hardworking hands.

As to hooks—especially over the door—they are so handy in bathrooms, closets, laundry rooms, or other areas where space is tight and clutter gathers. Decorative hooks can add a lot of panache and even help make a pseudo "mud room" in an entryway that's ever ready to hold jackets, backpacks, hats, and umbrellas.

Kitchen duty to kitchen beauty

I have a small kitchen and invested in an inexpensive rolling kitchen cart. It's perfect for extra counter space. I also put on it all we need for dinner and roll it right up to the dining table so I don't have to run back and forth between the dining room and kitchen. My kids think it's neat—like a busboy cart. I also splurge on graphically beautiful or whimsical paper goods and store them on the bottom of the cart. My five-year-old Tori (our "artiste") loves to choose the patterns we'll use at dinnertime and that helps her get into the "table setting mood." My fourteen-year-old son is also happy because he can toss all of the dirty dishes onto the cart when we are done. Voilà! No more gnashing of five-year-old teeth when it's time to get dinner on, and no more sullen teen when it's time to clean up (undoing all the family bonding we've just done over dinner)!

In case you're experiencing some household or lifestyle angst, I hope my Everyday Epiphanies will help inspire you to make an "about face." If you're anything like me, at the very least, you'll be a lot less cranky.

*Ask where the good way is, and walk in it,
and you will find rest for your souls.*
JEREMIAH 6:16 NIV

Chapter 47

The Clutter Cutter

When our family moved from Georgia to Texas, I had a ten-year-old son and a one-year-old daughter, and at thirty-eight, I already felt like an "old" mom.

A few months—and a red stripe across a pregnancy test—later, I had definitely (albeit unwittingly) sealed my fate as a "midlife mom." *No matter,* I consoled my aging, sagging self. *I'll just find some nice, advanced-in-years moms to hang out with.*

The problem was, in the town we settled in, "older moms" my age with babies were not exactly coming out of the tumbleweeds. My vision of hanging out with slightly wrinkled, pudgy, and graying moms gave way to a harsher reality.

Most moms with children the same age as mine were not only ten years younger than I, but twenty pounds lighter—and had a knack for wardrobe assembly, hair design, and nail artistry that would give Paris Hilton a run for her family money.

Was I frustrated? *Yes.* Did I try to move to another town with more "midlife moms"? *Yes.* Did that work? *No.* Did I still need a friend? *Yes.*

At first I considered a total makeover, including carting around a Shih Tzu puppy dog in a pink rhinestone collar while grocery shopping. But I figured that wouldn't do much good if I were still wearing my Big Bird T-shirt and Walgreen flip-flops.

Enter Tiffany Demien. God placed this young mother just a few streets from my house and in my Sunday school class. Better yet, she had daughters near the ages of mine. Nice assets, nice gal. Yes, she was about ten years younger, twenty pounds lighter, and fashion-savvy, but I was about to find out that she was also my saving grace.

With two very young daughters and millions of tiny pieces of toys—from Polly Pocket shoes and handbags, to stuffed animals and baby dolls—I soon found my midlife energy waning, and my house becoming increasingly ill-managed. If I weren't picking up toys or raking them into mounds, I was keeping laundry at bay, and losing the battle with most of it bulging out of the laundry room door.

I soon learned that my newfound friend Tiffany had a cottage industry as a "clutter cutter." She rolled up her sleeves, and dared to spelunk into the dark caverns of my laundry closet, kitchen cabinets, and bedroom closet. She began by yanking *every single thing* out. "A clean slate," she declared with glee, "is where we begin."

Her energy level picked up at the prospect of my new clutter-free existence. "Isn't this *fun*!" she'd sing while *my* energy level fell to that of Eeyore. "How will we *ever* get this back together?" I'd moan while pitching "stuff" into either the trash or a "keep" bin.

We *did* get it back together—gloriously back together. Now *I* was the one singing—every time I opened a beautifully arranged clutter-free cabinet or closet.

I thank God almost every day, not only for Tiffany's clutter cutting skills, but for the way she makes me feel totally at home in her presence—that "put your feet up and be yourself" kind of "at home feeling." Wasn't God good *not* to let me move?

So often when we think we know exactly what we need, God knows better. While we may not need literal "clutter cutting," He seems to know when we need emotional or spiritual clutter cutting—and He has a real knack for placing just the right people in our lives at just the right times. Isn't He something?

A friend loves at all times.
PROVERBS 17:17

Chapter 48

Near Misses

How many of us free-spirited women have had that most unfunny experience I refer to as a Near Miss—a time when you felt God was telling you to do a certain thing and you kept your focus on the bull's-eye, but when you let your arrow soar, God moved the target—leaving you holding your bow and scratching your head. At that point you probably felt like God had—let's see, how do I put this—"slipped out the back, Jack" (or in this case, Jehovah), and took the target with Him.

Recently a woman e-mailed me with a real heart-tugger of a Near Miss:

Out of Africa

Some years ago I felt a murmur in my heart calling me to missions. The murmur soon became a roar, and the door swung wide open for my new God-adventure—even to the details of a Nigerian named Moses asking me to work for him as he established a Bible school in his homeland. Financially, the Lord provided a buyer for my car and friends rented my home.

On the day of my departure, I was abuzz with excitement as I left all that was familiar to me to begin a new life with God as my only companion. I arrived at Lagos, the capital of Nigeria, where masses of people clogged the streets. Farmers herded sheep and goats through the main city thoroughfares, and I saw scenes of poverty at every turn. It was eye-opening and sobering, but I was determined to make a difference.

I found a home to rent with no running water, cockroaches the size of my thumb, and sporadic outages of electricity. But I soon acclimated to my new surroundings.

I went to work with Moses while aggressively praying for the Lord to continue to guide me. However, as weeks passed, I heard strange rumors regarding my relationship with my Nigerian brother. He had told others that God had sent me to be his bride. Somehow God hadn't copied me in on that memo! I also found out that the job Moses had promised me was only temporary. I frantically called my pastor in the United States, and he counseled me to come home right away.

When I returned, I was so embarrassed. After all, I had quit my job, sold my car, and rented out my home. It was humbling to explain to friends and family that my "calling" was a Near Miss from becoming a mail-order bride who had paid her own postage!

My friends invited me to move back into my home with them until they could find an apartment. The person who bought my car had not made payments, so I got my car back. I eventually got my old job back, too. Even though I returned bewildered, not understanding why God had allowed me to endure this In and Out of Africa experience, I was grateful for His presence and provision as I returned home.

I've since found my real calling. I now work with a company that provides bookkeeping and financial support to Christian organizations, churches, and nonprofit companies. I also keep financial records for a prominent evangelist who travels the world speaking about Jesus' saving grace.

And honestly, it's pretty wonderful not

having to wonder if my toaster will work or not, or where my next tub of warm bathwater will come from, or if the cockroaches are performing Riverdance on my kitchen floor.

Although I can't promise that we won't experience Near Misses, listening to the happy-ending stories of other believers is extraordinarily helpful. Often spiritual clouds do have silver linings, even if it takes awhile for the Son to reveal them.

When Moses' hands grew tired. . .Aaron and Hur held his hands up. . .so that his hands remained steady till sunset. So Joshua overcame the Amalekite army with the sword.
EXODUS 17:12–13

Chapter 49

The Death of Fun

Sometimes it's not easy being unconventional. The main problem is that I so often feel boxed in by "convention," that I end up living with more angst than what is probably recommended by the Mental Health Association.

For example, last summer our family was hitting a wall. After living seventeen years on the East Coast in close proximity to all things fun, trendy, and beautiful (i.e., Chesapeake Bay, Colonial Williamsburg, Blue Ridge Mountains within a close drive), we now found ourselves in Texas suburbia with great schools and nice folks, but not much to do unless you like to crawdad fish.

Not to rain on anyone's small-town parade, but

tying a raw chicken heart on a string and tossing it into a muddy creek isn't exactly my idea of a good time. Unless perhaps there's a Starbucks kiosk within walking distance of the bait shack, then I'm all over that—waders, a cup of coffee in one hand, string in the other. Polly put the kettle on—we're having crawfish for dinnah!

We were forty minutes from civilization and culture, so when faced with strapping our young and restless into car seats as the world turned ugly inside the van for the other passengers, we rarely ventured out, and thus became "town bound." After three years as residents, our greatest social achievement was that we were on a first-name basis with the Wal-Mart cashiers.

Add to that, my husband's hour-long commute through downtown Dallas that infringed upon our nightly family time, and we were slowly but steadily becoming a stuck-in-a-rut, disconnected family. As a humor writer, it pains me to pen this, but. . .our family was becoming. . .*boring*.

So, as I was contemplating our plight, I came up with an idea.

My husband says he could make a replica of Noah's ark if he had a wooden nickel made of gopher bark for every time I said, "Honey, I have an idea." But because of that fun-fueled pilot light of his, he's learned to lend me an ear, even if some ideas crawl right on through his brain and exit out the other side, like those earwigs you see in horror flicks.

Anyway, I suggested that we conduct an "experiment" to help revive our sagging sense of humor and adventure. The remedy? Take out a three-month lease on an apartment near endorphin-infusing venues in Dallas, halfway between our sub-suburban home and my husband's job. An urban getaway, if you will, our "little cabin in the city." We calculated the cost at roughly what we would spend on a week-long Florida vacation. But this way we would have three months of mini vacations to take on a whim, and we would finally come to know a great city that we were clueless about.

So we began making regular escapes, even midweek overnights to Big D or "Dow–ass" as my girls call it. Actually my teen, Trevor, calls it that, too, because, well, it's fun to say a bad word and not get called on the carpet for it.

In the beginning, there were protests from the rear seats of my minivan regarding the forty-minute drive into the city. Four-year-old Tori would wail, "I just want to go to Wal-Mart!"

Two-year-old Whitney would ask with excruciating regularity and repetition, in her emerging Texas accent, "Are we day–yer?" FYI: All one-syllable words are pronounced with two syllables in these parts, because, of course, "everything's bigger in Texas."

Note to knuckle-rapping obsessive-compulsive grammarians: "these parts" as well as "these here parts" are bona fide pronouns for the great state according to the Texas dictionary. Read it and weep, babie! (Am I driving you crazie?)

On the first occasion of dissent, I pulled over the van, careened my neck over the back of the seat with a rotation radius close to Linda Blair's in *The Exorcist*, and with a voice eerily similar, screeched "Everybody pipe down! We are going to expand our horizons and start having some fun if it *kills* me!"

As the girls' mouths closed, their eyes opened, looking like unblinking fried eggs. Had they possessed a more sophisticated vocabulary, I'm sure they would have muttered out the sides of their mouths, "Mom has really flipped her lid this time."

Well, this lid-flipper is happy to report that after only five minutes in the children's area of the Dallas Museum of Art, Tori was flitting from one hands-on activity to the next and proclaiming with glee, "Mom, I *love* this place!" Add to that several rousing jaunts to the children's museum and Slappy's Puppet Playhouse, and well, can you say, "Wal-*Who*?"

If we constantly tap down those unconventional voices and ideas, we may miss the opportunity to experience not only new things, but also God himself. Ideas and risk taking are a part of life, and I think a part of vibrant spirituality. As long as we're not elbowing God or other close sources of wisdom out of the scenario, it can be very rewarding to jump off a God-adventure cliff. Just hold on tight to His hand and maintain eye contact during the freefall!

Without faith it is impossible to please God, because anyone who comes to him must believe that he exists and that he rewards those who earnestly seek him.
HEBREWS 11:6

Chapter 50

My Cousin Jamie

My cousin Jamie frequently gets into crazy situations with her six kids. She's also managed to get through some very difficult low-income periods of her life with grace, good humor, and a double dose of pure charm. Angels watch over her and her large, eclectic crew for sure.

Now Jamie & Co. don't *mean* to get into crazy situations, but crazy situations seem to follow them wherever they go. Jamie wrote my mom about a tale involving this family of seven making their way around Houston's bustling thoroughfares in a decrepit old station wagon:

Aunt Ruthie, you remember how steep Mom

and Dad's driveway is? A driver needs to back out nice and easy, but I always forget and hit the dip and knock my license plate off. Before long my license plate was in such bad shape I couldn't screw it back on. So I arranged with Dolly and Roxie [teens with Down syndrome] that they would sit in the backseat of the station wagon facing backward and watch for policemen. When they saw one, they were to hold the license plate in the window.

This worked pretty well for a while, and Dolly and Roxie were so proud of themselves for their vigilance and excellence in a job well-done. But of course, one day I was stopped by a traffic policeman. When he came to my window, he looked into the back of the car, winced, and scratched his head. "Wow, you have quite a crew here!" he observed in a nice tone.

I immediately started explaining what had happened to my license plate.

"Ma'am," he interrupted politely. "Actually, you were speeding."

"I was?" I wasn't faking surprise. I had no idea. From the backseat, six-year-old Andy was getting worried and expressed his concern to Martha Kate. "Marfa, dat man has a gun. Is he a bad man?"

"No, he nice. He nice, Andy," MK replied.

I turned around to reinforce Martha's

information. *"Don't worry, Andy. He's nice. Policemen are nice."*

When I turned back to the officer, he was looking closely at my inspection sticker, which, to my surprise, had expired. Then he asked for my driver's license and proof of insurance. The license was easy, but I rummaged through my purse for the proof of insurance (he was tapping his fingers on the car window now, his niceness beginning to wane), then I looked through the pockets on the doors, and finally under the front seats. No proof of anything, except that I was not a member of Neatniks Anonymous.

Finally I drummed up my best smile and shrugged my shoulders, going for that innocent Shirley Temple look. I guess he hadn't seen any of Curly Top's movies, because he didn't pinch my cheeks endearingly or even smile. Instead, he handed my driver's license back to me.

"Did you know that's expired, too?" The poor guy looked very serious, seeming to struggle within himself about what to do with the wagon driven by Wacko Mom with six kids. Finally he made his decision.

"Okay, lady," he sighed heavily, "I'm gonna give you a warning this time, but (his voice had a pleading parental tone) you really need to get these things taken care of."

As we pulled back into traffic, I heard

Dolly tell Roxie, "We did just what we were supposed to do, Roxie. We did real good with the license plate. Didn't we, Jamie?"

With busy lives and hectic schedules, it's easy for some of us to become downright inept—at least for a time—until we can regroup or have enough money to deal with bills, overdue inspection stickers, or expired licenses! It's a rare but wonderful feeling when a kindhearted soul understands that we don't intend to get off track, and offers us a little grace. It may not happen often, but when it does, we can be certain that Someone's looking out for us, just like Dolly and Roxie looked out for Jamie.

For he will command his angels concerning you
to guard you in all your ways.
PSALM 91:11

Chapter 51

You've Got a Friend

Even in my earliest memories of playing on the sandy playground of Wimbish Elementary School in first grade, I can remember being nice to those who were less socially accepted by my peers. That's not so much a sign of great character—how could it be at age six? Perhaps it was because I tended to care how people felt and had parents who taught me that people need at least one person they can call a friend, or *pretend* is their friend!

So during my public school days, while I was not exactly Ms. Popular, I was somewhere in the middle of the Kid Caste System. (And, by the way, moms, isn't it frightening how early our children become aware of this very real system? Who's "in" and who's "out" is often defined by fashion more than personality, at least with girls!)

In first grade, I remember a red-haired class-mate who, for some reason, didn't get along well with most of the class. She was edgy and irritable with most kids, but perhaps they egged her on. However, Carla took to me like a "sick kitten to a warm brick" as my Grannie used to say. Although I wasn't crazy about Carla sitting next to me at circle time, I didn't hate it—or her.

However, the peer pressure mounted the day she came to school wearing a toboggan with the slogan "Ditch Witch" plastered across the forehead. (I later learned it was her father's place of employment, a company that made trenching machines.) Even so, I hung in there at least at circle time. But at recess, I tried to forge my own way with other friends, hoping Carla would do the same.

I don't remember any other serious social chal-lenges until high school. Robert was skinny as a skeleton, had a bad rep for being obnoxious, and lived in a trailer park. Robert and I were in the same health class, and he was questioning my character: Was I a socially impartial, nice, Christian girl, or was I "one of them"—a social snob? He challenged me to go out with him, and I accepted the chal-lenge, with safeguards.

One day at lunch hour, I stood with Robert in front of my high school in view of God and *everybody* waiting for his mom to come and take us to lunch. I wish I could say I was more concerned about what God would think, but I was truthfully more concerned about what "everybody" would think. Robert's mother mercifully showed up on time, but less mercifully in her rust brown station wagon. I think it was brown; it could have just been rust.

I remembering thinking, *This is not my finest hour!* But in a matter of moments, after being hit with the reality of someone else's more difficult reality (torn upholstery, no A/C, no. . .class), I was glad I'd accepted my schoolmate's invitation.

Robert's mom was overweight, with unkempt hair and a couple of missing teeth. Even so, she was pleasant, chatty, and seemed to enjoy our time together. Her enthusiasm was contagious, and I soon felt upbeat as well (after all, Burger Basket had *the* best BBQ sandwich in town!). As young as I was, I also noticed something in her eyes—a softness that alluded to gratitude, I think. Perhaps she was thankful that I was genuinely interested in her and our conversation, and including Robert in our chat—who was a perfect gentleman and never asked me out again. Or maybe it was that she knew I had made her son's day, if even once, by venturing over teen social barriers. Maybe that was my finest hour in high school after all.

In today's "hip" and "socially adept" social climates, it can be hard to step out of our familiar circles and reach out to someone who needs a friend, if even for a morning or a short season until they can find their own social footing. Most of us are terribly busy, but in the din of chatter before Sunday school class starts, or at a reception or club meeting, you might discover someone who feels like he or she doesn't fit. Someone may need to hear our friendly "hello."

This may feel uncomfortable at first, but when we take that first step toward being a welcoming person, we often find that when we give, we also receive—often in unexpected ways. After all, if *everybody* isn't watching, God is, and we can be sure *He* is pleased.

Let brotherly love continue.
Be not forgetful to entertain strangers:
for thereby some have entertained angels unawares.
HEBREWS 13:1–2 KJV

Chapter 52

End Game

Back in 1996 I walked into a Barnes and Noble bookstore in Chesapeake, Virginia, and pulled from the shelves a hardback book weighing roughly five pounds, with a red glossy jacket. The title? *The Writer's Market.*

That day I took my first baby steps into the writing world. I researched companies that would look at ideas for greeting cards, and I took a stab at writing some. I had a lot of fun but got bogged down in the process of sending my work out into the Greeting Card Cosmos, only to have them returned, sometimes six months after their launch. I began to calculate what I could expect in compensation if I stuck with the process: roughly five bucks. A year.

I had to muster a lot of emotional courage to walk into that bookseller and pay twenty-five dollars for a trade book when I wasn't even in the trade. I remember thinking, *Who are you to think that of all the people who would like to write for income, you can beat the odds?*

Ten years later, I'm struck with mixed emotions about where writing has taken me. Like the poet, Elizabeth Browning, let me begin with a "How Do I Love Thee?" ode to writing:

First of all, writing has been a journey of courage and belief. Courage to defy the naysayers and odds, and belief that God could make a way if it were good for His purposes.

Second, writing has been an unending "object lesson" as it reveals what's really important in my life. At first I was enamored with the thought of becoming a published writer. I was high on the idea of hanging out in Starbucks or Barnes and Noble with pen and paper and basking in the aroma of my success. I saw myself wearing black rectangular-shaped glasses, faded leather clogs, chatting it up with all the beautiful people in the neighborhood. Then God moved me out of that neighborhood and taught me a lot about "substance over style." At times I had to type with one hand while balancing a nursing baby with the other, while living in a hood filled with scary people instead of beautiful people.

Finally, after writing a small book of inspirational

humor, I've learned what an insignificant speck I am, and what an incomprehensibly personal being *God* is in the lives of His children.

Many times I felt low about an attitude I had, and then I'd receive an e-mail from a reader. Often she had been near giving up on connecting with God. Then she somehow reconnected with Him through laughter and realizing that she was not alone in her "crazy moments" when life felt over-whelmingly hard.

Tonight was one of those "feeling low" times for me again. So much so, that I hesitated to write about it. *What might people think,* I wondered, *if they knew how discombobulated I really feel much of the time?* Then I reasoned, *Well, they might relate, or feel sorry for me (and better about themselves!), or they might pray for me.* I figured it was a win-win-win, so here goes.

I spent the day excavating the kitchen and family room. Turns out I have a sink. And a sofa. I worked like a giant mole (looked like one, too—PMS does that to me) making "mounds" around the house. Mostly the mounds were laundry, but I also created Basket Hill—five baskets filled with everything from receipts to preschool papers and art (the guilt!), to candy wrappers and unidentifiable gunk in various stages of decay. The Mount of Suitcases was visible by the stairwell—four of them in various sizes from our Easter weekend away.

I was a week away from deadline, and although I've changed the status of our living quarters from High Risk to Elevated Risk (of breaking our necks by tripping over mounds or contracting rabies from a PMSing Mole Mom), it occurs to me, *I haven't written a word today.* Panicked and highly irritable, I tossed the kids into the van (and that's not a metaphor). Met my poor husband (that *is* a metaphor. Kind of. He has money, but the quality of his life with me lately is poor), and transferred the kids into his car. I drove to the nearest Barnes and Noble in search of drugs, er, caffeine. Coffee secured and sanity on the way, I looked for the nearest outlet to plug my finger into. . .I mean plug my laptop into.

Thankfully I don't have to, with the flair of another famous poet, decide tonight whether "to write or not to write, *that* is the question." But just in case *Laugh Yourself to Sleep* is not only a sequel, but a swan song, you'll know where I'll be: living the simple life. At home with a sparkling porcelain sink, folding laundry atop my long-lost sofa, enjoying the fleeting early years of my daughters' lives and my son's last years in high school before he leaves for college, and lounging with my husband in our overstuffed chaise.

Whether this is "till we meet again" or "farewell," please know that I am honored beyond words that you chose to read my book out of the millions out there vying for your attention. Believe me, I know the competition is stiff—I'm here looking at it at Barnes and Noble Booksellers.

God be with you and yours. May you find contentment and happiness whether your life is simple or complicated or somewhere in between.

I have learned the secret of being content. . .whether living in plenty or in want. I can do everything through him who gives me strength.
PHILIPPIANS 4:12–13

Permissions

Stories of, and quotations by, friends
and acquaintances of the author
have been used by permission.

Excerpts from Terry Lindvall's *The Mother of
All Laughter: Sarah and the Genesis of Comedy*
(Nashville: Broadman & Holman, 2003)
are used by permission of the publisher.